Making money is hard...but Ben Nash makes it so much easier. His approach to investing is just so sensible. Replacing your salary means independence. Achieve that and your financial stress fades. It can literally change your life forever.

— David 'Kochie' Koch, Australia's original Money Nerd and Chairman, Pinstripe Media

When Ben comes on *The Morning Show*, we know he's going to demystify the normally confusing and overwhelming world of finance. He cuts through all the hysteria and hype with easily understood language and solutions, which is the approach he takes in *Replace Your Salary by Investing* — a must read for anyone looking to be smarter with their money.

— Larry Emdur, host of *The Chase Australia* and co-host of *The Morning Show Australia*

So inspiring and helpful! Great game plan. Ben's expertise is clear, but his writing is even clearer. Highly recommended.

— Derek Sivers, Entrepreneur, Investor, Author

Most people spend their lives craving true financial freedom. Ben's book will show you how to start (and keep!) investing...so you can stop dreaming about it and start living it!

— Jessica Brady, Financial Adviser and Speaker

The world of personal finance and investing can be confusing and overwhelming, which creates a big barrier to people doing what they need to do to take control of their money. In *Replace Your Salary by Investing*, Ben breaks down the barriers and explains the building blocks of money and investing in a way that's easy to understand and easy to action, helping readers to move forward with confidence.

— Brendan Malone, CEO, Raiz Invest

Financial independence will be a defining theme of the next century. *Replace Your Salary by Investing* gives you the plan to get there faster and easier through simple, practical tips and hacks that actually work. Ben cuts through the noise around money that's often overwhelming to deliver clear, actionable steps to take you from where you are to where you want to be. This book is a must read for anyone looking to level up their money game.

— Nick Nicolaides, Co-founder, Pearler

In *Replace Your Salary by Investing*, Ben breaks down complex topics into practical, step-by-step tips that are easy for readers to understand and easy to action. Ben avoids the common jargon and confusing terminology that can be overwhelming to help people build confidence around the most innovative next steps to move forward with their money. Highly recommended for anyone looking to make their money work harder and simplify important investing fundamentals.

— Clint Newton, CEO, Rugby League Players' Association

REPLACE YOUR SALARY BY INVESTING

Save More, **Invest** Smart and **Maximise Your Money**

Ben Nash

WILEY

First published in 2023 by John Wiley & Sons Australia, Ltd
Level 4, 600 Bourke St, Melbourne, Victoria 3000, Australia

Typeset in ACaslonPro 11pt/15pt

ISBN: 978-1-394-17665-6

 A catalogue record for this
book is available from the
National Library of Australia

Cover design by Alex Ross Creative

Disclaimer
The material in this publication is of the nature of general comment and
general advice only. It is not personal advice as it does not take into account
the reader's personal circumstances, needs and objectives. It is not intended
to provide specific guidance for particular circumstances and it should not
be relied on as the basis for any decision to take action or not take action
on any matter which it covers. Readers should obtain professional advice
where appropriate, before making any such decision. To the maximum
extent permitted by law, the author and publisher disclaim all responsibility
and liability to any person, arising directly or indirectly from any person
taking or not taking action based on the information in this publication.

Contents

This book is dedicated to my three favourite (and best performing)
investments, Yang, Margot, and Olivia.

About the author

If you're not familiar with me or Pivot Wealth, you might be wondering who I am and why I'm the best person to help you replace your salary by investing.

I'm a financial adviser and the founder of Pivot Wealth, a money management company that helps people invest smarter to create a life not limited by money. I'm deeply passionate about helping people make better money choices so they can live a better life.

Through my work I draw on my practical experience to simplify the often overwhelming area of money by distilling complex tactics and strategies into simple, practical, actionable steps. I'm also a speaker, podcaster, writer, TikTok'er, financial educator, a regular writer for News.com.au, and author of the book *Get Unstuck*.

My content is authentic, practical, to the point, and jargon-free to drive rapid implementation and rapid results.

Unlike the majority of financial advisers in Australia, I've chosen to focus on people in their 30s and 40s still building their wealth towards financial independence. Also in contrast to traditional financial advice, my work has a strong focus on lifestyle alongside money outcomes, something I feel is crucial to drive a money plan that will actually work for you.

I'm a finance geek at heart and have studied extensively in the area of finance including two Master's degrees and my undergraduate study, alongside a number of specific financial advice professional qualifications. That being said, it's primarily from my practical experience that the concepts in this book are drawn.

Both myself and Pivot Wealth have been formally recognised, named as part of the Financial Standard Top 50 most Influential Financial Advisers in Australia for six consecutive years, the Independent Financial Adviser Industry Thought Leader of the Year, Innovator of the Year (twice), Association of Financial Advisers Excellence in Education Award, Best Client Servicing Financial Adviser in Australia, Best Client Servicing Financial Advice Firm, Marketing Program of the Year, and Pivot Wealth has been listed as part of the Australian Financial Review's 100 Fastest Growing Companies in Australia. We have also been recognised as award finalists for Wellness Program of the Year, Self Licensed Firm of the Year, Digital Advice Strategy of the Year, Women's Community Program of the Year, SME Employer of the Year, and part of the AFR Boss Best Places to Work.

I've partnered with leading organisations to deliver financial education content, including working with the National Rugby League (NRL) to create and deliver their financial education program for all professional male and female NRL players. In addition, we've delivered content for the Australian Government, Newscorp, Glaxosmith Kleine, WeWork, Pearler, SelfWealth, Raiz Invest, VoltBank, Work-Shop, and Publicis Media, among others.

In addition to my work at Pivot, I'm a co-founder of Ensombl, Australia's biggest community of financial advisers dedicated to driving the positive evolution of financial advice in Australia and around the world.

Having advised and coached over a thousand people directly through one-on-one financial advice, worked indirectly with thousands more, and presented to over 100 000 people through live events, I've found what really works (and what doesn't).

When you have a solid understanding of what's really possible you become empowered to confidently make the smartest money choices. The feeling of being empowered, the relief that comes from knowing your money is sorted, and the elimination of money stress is something I passionately believe every person should have and something I feel very privileged to help people achieve.

Introduction

When I finished high school, the world of money was a complete unknown to me. I'd never heard of financial planning. I'd never set up a budget. I knew nothing about investments. In fact, I didn't even know anyone who worked in finance.

A few years later my nan gave me a book that opened my eyes to the world of personal finance and investing. I was immediately hooked.

In the two decades since, I've been on a mission to learn as much as I possibly can about investing and how to be successful with money.

Initially, this was driven by a largely selfish motivation to pick up as many tips, tricks and hacks as I could to help me on my own money journey. I wanted to do well financially so I could create the freedom to live my own ideal lifestyle. On discovering financial advising as a career path, I was immediately drawn in by the fact that my job allowed me to help other people do the same.

I've had the opportunity to help thousands of people with their money. I can't claim to have 'seen it all', because I'm still constantly being surprised, but I have seen a lot.

I'm a pretty curious kind of guy, and I'm always looking out for any hacks that can give me or our clients at Pivot Wealth an advantage. When I talk to people about their money I pay close attention, and I've noticed patterns. Whenever I talk to someone who has done exceptionally well with their money, I'm keen to learn how they got there. As Tony Robbins put it, 'success leaves clues', and there are things that successful people do differently.

On the flip side, whenever I talk to someone who is really struggling with their money or is in financial trouble, I take the time to uncover and understand where things went wrong. In this way I've found the common mistakes people make that lead to trouble.

It's the things I've learned from this practical experience that I want to share in this book. I'll help you to learn from other people's mistakes so you can avoid making them yourself. And you'll hear about the principles and strategies that people doing well with their money have applied, and what they do to maintain their success.

Financial security, independence, freedom—a lot of different terms are used to signify success with money. For me, it comes down to replacing your salary, and investing is how you get there.

When your investments are sufficient to replace your ideal salary, you no longer need to work for an income to fund the lifestyle you want. Importantly, this frees up your time, which is the driver of true freedom.

When you don't *have* to work, you may still *choose* to work. I love what I do, and it doesn't matter how much money I have, I'll still want to work on interesting things where I feel like I can be productive and help people.

The key is that you're then working out of choice. If you want to take six months off to travel, do charity work or help out a family member, you can choose to do so. I think everyone should have this freedom. And my experience has shown me that it is within your reach too, *if* you go about it the right way. I'm going to show you exactly how.

In the pages that follow I'll guide you, step by step, through exactly what you need to know to replace your salary by investing. I'll cover the building blocks of your finances, how to set up a solid financial foundation, and how to invest effectively and grow your wealth through shares, property, crypto and super. And we'll examine how you can be smarter with your tax and set up a rock-solid game plan to maximise your money and get ahead faster.

If you're new to money, it can seem overwhelming. But it shouldn't be, because the reality is that the principles of money success are simple. You need to spend less than you earn so you can save more. You need to invest consistently, and you need to use the rules to your advantage so you can optimise your results.

But just because it's simple, it doesn't mean it's easy.

There's a lot of psychology that impacts what you do with your money — how you manage it, how you spend it, how you invest it and how you plan with it. To create true money success, you need not only to *know* the principles of money success, but to manage your money so you can consistently *follow* them.

As with anything important, consistency is key. You should build good habits and tactics that will actually work for you. You have to manage your money in a way that drives an ongoing focus on what's working and what's not, so you can refine your approach and strategy over time. And you need to avoid drifting off track and making mistakes that lead to setbacks.

There are no shortcuts to money success.

Even winning Powerball or scoring a big inheritance won't do it. Sure, this will boost your financial position quickly, but if you don't have the right approach to lasting money success this boost will be short-lived, and ultimately you'll end up back in the purgatory of money mediocrity. This is why so many people who come into significant money aren't able to make it last.

To create sustainable, long-lasting, real money success, you need to get 'good at money'. You need to know enough to make good money choices, to know not only how to choose good investments but how to choose the right investments *for you*.

There are many different ways to be right with money, but there's only one right way for you. The right money moves for you depend on you — on where you're at now, how you want your situation to play out over time, what's important to you, and how you feel about different risks and trade-offs.

There's no 'one right way' to be successful with money that will work for everyone, but there is a right *approach* to making money and investing decisions.

You first need to understand the (not so basic) basics of different money and investing options, how these options work, their benefits and trade-offs, and how they might work for you. From there, you need to integrate them into your lifestyle today and how you want your lifestyle to change over time, making sure they fit and that your risks are well managed.

These elements and this process is what I'll unpack for you in the pages that follow. I won't ruin the surprise, but let me tell you the results are worth it.

When you get your approach right, you'll be able to confidently make financial decisions and investments that will deliver the financial outcomes you want, and fit the lifestyle you want to live. With your risks managed you won't get caught short. And importantly, you'll be clear on where you're headed with your money and on the results you should expect over time.

I hope you're as excited to learn as I am to share.

One final word of warning before we get started. There's always a good reason to *not* take action. Perhaps you have a holiday coming up, or a child finishing school or day care, or you're waiting for your next pay rise. There can be any number of compelling reasons why you feel it might be better to put off your next steps with money.

I'm not going to sugarcoat it. Money success and replacing your salary by investing does mean making some sacrifices. You need to save and invest today money that you could otherwise be spending on things that make you feel really good today. But those moments are short-lived, and if you're constantly chasing maximum short-term satisfaction, you're sabotaging your long-term success and happiness.

Putting off taking serious action with your money now simply means you're going to have to do more later. You'll have to sacrifice more in the future, saving and investing more to arrive at the same position. Or worse, you'll have to make sacrifices around where you'll end up.

There's work to be done, but the juice is worth the squeeze.

When you go through the process of taking control of your money, there's an immediate shift. You gain clarity on what you're working towards and confidence on your next steps, and any stress around money is reduced.

Every single person I've ever helped has told me they wish they had started sooner. But here's the thing: if the best time to take action was 10 years ago, the second-best time is today.

Happy reading.

CHAPTER 1

Build your money muscle

Money isn't easy.

There, I said it. You knew it. I knew it. But not a lot of people talk about it. And because we don't talk about money, it's easy to fall into the trap of thinking *everyone* else has it more together than you do.

They don't.

There's so much confusion out there when it comes to money. In Australia there are thousands of different investment options and service providers, banking solutions, crypto investment opportunities, super funds — the list goes on. Figuring out which options are best is hard.

Then, even if you manage to work through these options, you need to create a smart money plan that fits with the many specific variations of your lifestyle into the future.

So yeah, money can be tricky. But the good news is that you don't need to be an expert from day 1.

If your aim is to achieve serious money success, by the time you get to the finish line you *will* need to have a lot of money knowledge and skills. But you don't need those skills to get started. The main building block of money success is investing, and you'll need some knowledge to get started, but you won't need to know it all.

For example, if you were to invest just $5000 in the next year, this money would grow to be worth $248 022 in 40 years' time based on the long-term Australian share market return of 9.8 per cent. You can see from this example the upside of getting started early, and the real cost of *not* taking action.

The fact that $5k invested this year will grow to almost a quarter of a million dollars over time shows that the downside of not investing is huge. For *every single year* you delay getting started, you're costing yourself six figures in lost wealth you'll never get back. You'll then need to play catch-up in the future, sacrificing more to arrive at the same position or having to compromise on your goals.

Imagining you need to be a money or investing expert *before* you get started often leads to the feeling of overwhelm, which in turn can result in getting stuck in the inaction trap.

Money is a muscle

Money is a muscle you build over time. As with any muscle exercise, you start with the basics, and as you grow and develop you get more complex and nuanced in your approach.

I do a lot of financial advice and education work with professional athletes, and through this work I've come to realise there's a lot of crossover between being an elite athlete and being elite with your money.

When you first start playing sport as a kid, you don't jump straight into a high-performance plan, a conditioning framework and all the other training routines a professional athlete does day in and day out. Instead, you focus on the basics. You do some running to get your physical fitness up. You do basic drills to help with your coordination. You take up exercises to build your strength and speed, maybe some push-ups or sprints. Then you rinse and repeat, building these skills. Regularly. For years. Over time you add more techniques and tactics to your training routines to raise your game.

When you watch an elite athlete perform, they make it look so easy. But what you don't see is the countless hours of practice over years, often decades. It's in this practice that skills are formed, honed and perfected.

Fast forward to the future, when you're crushing it with your money. You have all the skills you need, because you have put in the necessary practice to build your money muscle. And now *you* are making it look effortless.

But you're not there yet. Early on in your journey you just need to take the next step. You need to flex your money muscle to build it just a little so you can take on the next exercise, the next variation, to make the progress you're aiming for today.

Once you've achieved that you'll have learned some lessons and built some skills that will make whatever comes next easier. You can then set your next target and pursue that goal until you get there. At that point you'll have learned some more and added new skills to your tool kit, which in turn will help you move further forward.

You can see where this is going...

If you let it, thinking you need to be an expert from the start will prevent you from getting started. It will thwart any progress, blocking you from learning and growing your money muscle. Ultimately, it will stop you from building your money momentum.

How to build your money muscle

There are three things you need to do to build any muscle, including your money muscle.

First, you need a goal, something to aim for. In the early stages, you'll want it to be something relatively simple that you can achieve within the next 12 or, ideally, six months.

It could be something like building a certain amount of money in your emergency savings account, paying off that annoying credit card debt, or starting a share or investment portfolio.

The important thing here is that this goal is clear and your progress measurable. Specifically, you want to know whether or not you've achieved it. So a target such as 'doing better' or 'saving more' isn't as good as 'saving $1000' or 'reducing your debt by $1000'.

Next, you need to know what your next step is to make it happen. It's good to have great ideas and great plans for your money, but ideas without action are meaningless and ideas alone won't get you the *results* you want.

At this point you don't want to be overwhelmed by all the steps you have to take, you just want to be clear on the very next step. Then, once you take that step, you can refocus on what's next, and before you know it you'll be building momentum.

These first two steps are the biggest drivers of your initial action, but how well you do step 3 will dictate how much success you actually achieve. The third step is to check in on the progress you're making on your plan, and whether or not you're on track.

The importance of tracking your progress

If you're a high achiever, you may have noticed a tendency to focus on the things you want but don't yet have. It may be a certain amount in your savings or investments, an asset target, a property goal or a certain level of investment income.

If you're not yet exactly where you want to be, you focus heavily on the work you have left to do. In one way this is a good thing, because when you really want something you're more likely to work at it. But if you don't take the time to acknowledge and celebrate the progress you've made to get to where you are right now, you can find yourself feeling stressed as you fall short of where you want to be.

Instead of focusing on what's coming up, measure backwards: look at the progress you've made over the past month, three months, year, five years. You'll most likely be pleasantly surprised.

If buying this book is your first big positive step with money for a while, celebrate that. If you've been focused on your money for some time, look at the wins you've had over the recent past and celebrate them. We can park this thought for now, but know that celebrating your wins is an important way to drive your motivation moving forward.

As you implement the learnings from this book and make more progress with your money, you should schedule time to look back and acknowledge your money wins. This will help you see that the work you're putting in is worth it, and keep your motivation levels high as you move forward.

If when looking back you realise you're not entirely on track, that's not ideal, but it's also okay. Money plans don't work for three main reasons: you've done something wrong, there was something wrong with your plan, or something that was out of your control impacted your results. You'll want to figure out which one of these factors applies so you can address it. Once you do, you'll be clear on what you need to do to drive your forward momentum.

Is your current strategy the best one for you?

Three factors that will change over time can impact whether you're still doing the very best thing you can with your money.

First, what's going on with your money. Over time your income, spending and savings will change. You'll have some investments that perform really well and others that don't, and different financial opportunities will crop up.

The second factor that impacts your money strategy is what you want and what's important to you. This will include things like where you want to live, where you want to take your career and work, your family lifestyle, when and where you want to 'retire', and the people and causes you want to support.

As your wants change, you should be looking to your money strategy to make as many of them happen for you as possible.

The third element is what's going on in the world, notably in the financial and investment markets. How is the share market is performing? What's happening in the property market? How are interest rates tracking? What's going on in the economy and what does this mean for the outlook on investments.

As each of these three areas shifts and changes over time (and change they will), you need to check in on what you're doing with your money to make sure you stay on the front foot and are still making the right decisions and taking maximum advantage of your current financial position.

Money success—myth vs reality

Most people think that choosing good investments is the key to money success. Making good investments *is* important, but it's only a small part of what you need for real success.

Being truly successful with money is about investing the right amount at the right time. It's about optimising for tax. You want to use the right amount of leverage. You need a good debt strategy. You also need to have the right approach to your saving and day-to-day money management.

You must manage risk well and have a plan that never sees you forced to sell good investments at the wrong time. You need to have good goals and targets, and to keep yourself motivated to get there. In this way you build your confidence and avoid money stress.

Sure, choosing good investments is important, but it's less than half of what you need to get right to achieve your financial potential.

Urgent vs important

Success with money unfortunately isn't something that will just happen on its own. Money is *important*, but it's rarely *urgent*.

It's easy enough to not make the time today for your money without too much of an impact *today*. Just like skipping a session at the gym, treating yourself to a third helping of dessert, or not taking the time to do that bit of research or study to develop your professional skills or career, there's no immediate, earth-shattering impact.

But if you repeat these behaviours every day for years, things will start to decline. The decline will be slow at first, but if you let it reach a tipping point, things can deteriorate rapidly. Making the time to keep your money moving forward is something that's easy to put off for a tomorrow that never seems to come around.

On the flip side, once you start taking action you start building momentum. You start building habits and behaviours that drive results. These results then drive your motivation to keep going, and take your results to the next level.

There are interesting parallels between being money fit and being physically fit. Your past choices around your diet and exercise routines dictate your current level of physical fitness and health. It's easy to get out of shape, because inactivity and poor eating habits can make you feel good, at least temporarily. Making the time to work out is harder than skipping your workout for a Netflix and chill session, with some extra calories thrown in for good measure.

These poor habits lead to your not being as on top of your diet and exercise as you know you should be, and your physical fitness suffers as a result. Let this pattern set in, and it's easy to get way out of shape.

No matter where you're at, though, it's possible to turn things around. Once you decide to make your physical health a priority and start putting in the work to make it happen, you'll drive results.

Build new habits and behaviours that have a positive impact on your health, and you'll start making progress. It might seem slow at first, but it's there. Then with focus, and compounding over time, you start moving closer to where you want to be.

Keep this going and you'll eventually achieve your goals. Then you can start to think about your next level of goals, which may be beyond what you'd previously thought was even possible.

It's the same with money.

If you're already doing okay, giving this time and attention will take things to the next level. If you're a little out of shape, you need to rebuild habits and behaviours that will get things back on track.

Just as with your physical health, there are no shortcuts to money success. The financial equivalent of a fad diet or tummy tuck might deliver some quick results, but if you don't have the right foundation, approach, habits and behaviours, any benefits will be short-lived. You simply can't shortcut your way to real, long-term money success.

Money stages

Everyone's situation is unique, but there are some key stages we all go through with money.

Of course, it's common for people to progress through some stages without thinking too much about their approach to money or without taking their money success too seriously. If this happens, you can push through some of the stages without much thought or focus.

Here I'm more interested in what will happen with your money once you make a commitment to taking a serious approach to your progress and financial success.

Building wealth

The first stage of your journey to replacing your salary by investing is all about building your investments and wealth. How much wealth you build will be dictated by how much income you can generate from your investments and your lifestyle, so this stage is critical.

How soon you get on this path and how fast you progress along it will determine how far you can go, so give yourself some snaps for picking up this book and starting on your journey.

Winding back on your salary

On your journey to replacing your salary through investing, you'll reach a critical inflection point. This is the point at which you'll be able to start reducing your salary and relying more on the income generated by your investments.

Some people choose to push through this point, continuing to focus on earning employment income and building more wealth faster to get to the point of financial freedom sooner. The 'right' approach will depend on you, your personal goals and lifestyle, your career and what's really important to you.

Financial freedom

For me, once you have enough investments behind you to generate your ideal salary without your needing to work, you've reached nirvana. At this point you may decide to continue working, but this will be out of choice, not necessity. You may opt to take extended leave to pursue a passion or help causes important to you or your family.

The key here is *choice*.

The building blocks to getting there

There are some key building blocks that will get you through these stages, and knowing what they are ahead of time will help you feel more confident in the path you're taking.

Saving

The first stage is all about your savings and day-to-day money management. You want to set up your money so you're able to spend the money you want on your lifestyle today *and* save at a rate you're happy with. At this stage you also need to create a money management system and approach to make saving easy.

Being tactical with your saving and spending is crucial to all later stages of your money management. Nailing this step sooner will accelerate your progress.

Investing

Getting good at investing is important for long-term money success. Particularly in Australia, where we have a compulsory superannuation system, most people are already investing, but they do so without much knowledge or thought, letting their employer or super fund dictate the strategy.

Investing through shares (or more likely managed funds, ETFs or micro-investing) will help you build serious wealth over time, and small changes made early will have a massive impact in the future.

Chapter 3, on investing, describes how to get started investing and set up your investments for success.

Property and leverage

Property is the most effective way to grow your wealth, because when you buy property you're typically not just investing with your own money. When you borrow and then invest, so long as you choose your investment wisely and have a solid plan, you'll accelerate your progress far beyond what's possible using your savings alone.

But property debt entails significant risks that you must manage and manage well. So when it comes time for you to take this path, you'll want to have the other elements of your money sorted so you don't get caught out.

Financial wellbeing

In Australia and around the world, our levels of financial wellbeing are low. According to the 2022 Financial Wellness report from AMP, almost 3 million Australian workers are feeling moderate or severe levels of financial stress. One in five Australians report that financial stress impacts their productivity in the workplace, and 25 per cent of Australians report not enjoying life because of the way they're managing money.

These are scary stats and show the nonfinancial impact of falling short with your money management.

I've found there are three main elements you need to get right to achieve money wellbeing.

A clear plan

If you don't know where you're headed with your money, it's hard to build confidence. It's also impossible to know if you're doing enough, not enough or even too much.

It still blows me away how few people are clear on the actual financial trajectory they're currently on. What I mean by this is that most people aren't clear where they're likely to be financially in a month, a year, five years or later if they keep doing exactly what they're doing today.

Taking the time to map this out and understand how and where you're heading with your money will prompt an immediate shift. You'll generate instant feedback on whether what you're doing now is enough to get you to where you want to be, which allows you to course-correct if necessary and gives you peace of mind if you're on track.

If you need to change what you're doing to get to where you want to be with your money, the best time to do so is today. If you wait a week, a month or a year, you'll just need to do more.

A clear plan also helps build your confidence. Even if you're not 100 per cent on track, at least you can now start thinking about what you're going to change to make it happen.

Having a clear plan, and understanding that what you want is possible, will also increase your motivation. You'll realise that your goal is realistic and achievable, and this will motivate you to put in the work to get there.

A clear plan also works as a tool to help you start making smarter choices, because you'll be able to see the impact of making changes. You can look at how much you're investing, which investments you choose, different levels of borrowing and leverage, and different levels of spending. These all impact your financial trajectory differently, and understanding these differences is an important tool when making the best choices for you.

Know your unknowns

One of the biggest barriers to financial wellbeing is doubt and uncertainty. Because there are so many different aspects and elements to money, and because they can be so complicated and confusing, it's common to experience that niggling thought in the back of your mind that there's something you're missing that's going to lead to trouble.

In the early stages, when you're just getting started saving, your path is pretty clear. But as you start building some solid money momentum and your money progress accelerates, it's common to feel increasing doubt and uncertainty. The solution is to have your money approach sense-checked by a professional to eliminate uncertainty and doubt and deliver confidence.

A good professional will quickly see if there's something you're missing, something that might be slowing you down or holding you back, or something unknown bubbling away below the surface that could lead to trouble later on.

Knowing your unknowns will give you the peace of mind to go 'all in' on your money plan. You'll follow through to get the results you want faster, and you'll do so with more confidence.

Manage your risks

Risk is a good thing, because it's what makes you money. But if the risks are unknown or aren't managed well, they can cause you trouble. Some risks are obvious; others are less clear, like the lifestyle risk when purchasing a property where spending the wrong amount can force you to make serious lifestyle sacrifices.

If your risks aren't well managed, they can cost you money and cause setbacks that derail your money progress.

Risk often can't be eliminated altogether, but it can be managed and reduced. And *knowing* your key risks are managed goes a long way to reducing financial stress. As you're planning and executing your money moves, ensure that you understand the risks you're facing and that they're managed well.

Money psychology

The easy path with money is often the one that's most inconsistent with our money success. This happens because our thinking and psychology often push us towards what feels best in the moment, what's easiest or the comfort of the known.

If you want to achieve the best results from your money with the least amount of hard work, you should understand the money psychology hacks you can use to make your life easier.

We stick to defaults

Most of us, generally speaking, are lazy. We stick to our default patterns and behaviours, and don't stray too far into the unknown. We take the same route to the office every day. We follow the same routines at lunch. We go to the same place for coffee.

This happens because there's so much going on in our brains that to avoid driving ourselves crazy weighing up every single choice we face, we tend to do a lot of things without actively thinking about them. When it comes to your money this can be either a hack or a roadblock.

When talking to a new client about their money I ask how they're currently managing things to get a sense of their approach. A lot of people have set up fairly complicated systems for their money management: their income comes into one account; they split it out to different accounts, pay bills here, pay expenses there, save somewhere else. My head starts to spin.

The more you have to physically and manually do with your money, the more you're likely to get wrong, forget to do or give up on.

On the flip side, the more you can automate these processes, the closer you get to setting your default outcome to success. Automating your money management means that to get off track you'll need to actually interrupt or move away from your default strategy. This goes a long way to increasing your chances of getting the results you want from your money.

Parkinson's Law

A bunch of studies have shown that we tend to consume what we have available. The original work in this area was around the fact that when we have a task to complete, it tends to take however much time we have available.

If you need to do a work project or assignment in one month, it will take you a month. But if you need to complete it in a week, often you'll somehow meet that deadline.

The same principle has been applied to dieting, where it has been found that using smaller dinner plates reduces how much food we consume and is a very effective weight loss strategy.

This might seem strange, because we still have access to the same types and amounts of food, so we could eat just as much with a small plate by having multiple serves. But the thing is, we don't. We tend to consume what's in front of us. When something isn't immediately available, we stop consuming.

When it comes to money, your dinner plate is like your bank account: the more you have in easy reach, the more you're likely to consume. This is why I've worked with clients with super-strong, six-figure incomes who struggle to save as much as someone on minimum wage.

Put money out of sight and out of easy reach, and you'll be less likely to use it. This is why I like keeping the money for my bills away from my everyday spending money, I'm much less likely to spend money I can't see.

The power of barriers

Small barriers make a big difference. When it comes to your bank accounts, separating your different pots of money in different bank accounts, or keeping your savings in a different bank, leverages the power of small barriers. The same approach can be applied to other areas of your money.

Using multiple accounts won't stop you from blowing your budget, but it will force you to make a conscious choice and jump through a small hoop to get off track, which I've found will dramatically increase your chances of saving success.

Willpower is limited

Another group of studies can teach us some important lessons about money. Roy Baumeister is the godfather of research around willpower as a limited resource. His studies show that if we use too much willpower in one area of our lives, we won't have enough left to use in other areas.

In today's time-poor world, many of us must balance working hard in our careers, looking after family, trying to keep fit and healthy, investing in being a good partner and friend, and being financially responsible. Each of these areas requires willpower, because what's easy is the opposite of what will drive the outcomes you want. You've only got so much willpower you can use.

If you set yourself up to be tempted with your money *and* you're flexing your willpower in other areas in your life, you're more likely to give in to temptation. Instead, aim to set up your money in a way that doesn't need you to use a lot of willpower. Leverage the power of barriers, and automate your banking, saving and investing, to drastically increase your chances of money success.

THE WRAP

Everyone wants to be successful with money. We want it all—the epic lifestyle, the ability to work the way we want, and to help the people and causes we care about. All these things come at a cost, and the downside of living in an amazing country like Australia is that these things don't come cheap.

Particularly in the early stages of your money journey, getting to where you want to be can seem like an impossible challenge. You doubt what's possible and wonder whether there's some secret, better way to tackle things.

This doubt and uncertainty kills motivation, and can lead to inertia and inaction. Ultimately you miss out on the opportunity to drive the progress you want, creating an opportunity cost that will compound for decades to come. Don't fall into this trap!

The compounding impact over time you get from building good money habits is huge. Whether in relation to your health, wellbeing and fitness, your career or your relationships, small actions today will create opportunities tomorrow. Over time these opportunities get bigger and bigger, until before you know it your momentum is accelerating, making your progress seem almost effortless.

But habits work both ways, and letting bad habits compound over time will push you off track, sending you further and further away from where you really want to be. The longer you let bad habits continue, the harder it is to ditch them.

I'm not saying it's going to be easy, but I am saying the easiest and best time to make a change is today.

___

CHAPTER 2

Become a savings superstar

Spending money is way more fun than saving it.

This means that as a saver you're locked in an ongoing battle with your inner spender who craves the sweet, sweet pleasure hit you get from buying that new shiny object, splashing out on an experience or just paying for a convenience that will save you time.

At the same time, you know how much more quickly you get ahead when you save more money faster.

Early on your journey to replace your salary by investing, how much you save and invest will be the single biggest contributor to your rate of progress. And as important as it is while you're growing your money, once you've built your wealth being rock solid on your spending will ensure the money you have lasts.

The rule of thumb for how much wealth you need to replace your salary is to multiply the salary you want by 20. For example, if you want to replace an annual salary of $50k you need around $1 million in wealth. If you need to replace $100k, you need $2 million.

___

What this means is that the more you spend, the more wealth you need to cover your spending, and the longer it will take you to replace your salary by investing.

But saving isn't everything. An important part of true money success is enjoying the journey as well as the destination. True saving and money success is about saving well *while* living a lifestyle you love.

Most people could make drastic lifestyle sacrifices and save at a much faster rate, but to do so would mean 'wasting' years of their life that they could be enjoying more.

Note that some people are naturally drawn to living modestly, enjoying a simple lifestyle. If this is you, and you're already good at saving, well done. You can probably skip ahead to the next chapter. For everyone else, read on ...

Saving isn't easy. Life can be expensive, and there are so many nice things you can spend your money on. And money management can be complicated and confusing, making it hard to maintain your saving plan.

The good news is that there are a few hacks and tricks that can help you to save more and spend better. And even if you're one of those rare people who finds it easy to save, there are a few pro-level tactics I'll share that can help you take your savings game to the next level.

Saving challenges

There are three major saving challenges you'll need to overcome to become a savings superstar:

- **Changing money habits.** Easy spending behaviours often lead to the opposite of saving success.

- **Escaping the juggle.** It's common to have money moving around between different bank accounts without any real clarity on how much you're spending or saving.
- **Finding balance.** Saving at a rate you're happy with *while* living the life-style you want is hard.

Saving and spending habits

As already discussed, your money habits and behaviours will have a significant impact on your levels of saving success. These habits impact all areas of your money management but are particularly critical when it comes to your spending and saving.

Spending money is fun and brings immediate pleasure, so resisting the urge to spend can be challenging.

Add to this the fact that you're often saving money today to benefit you in the future, maybe many years in the future, and it gets even harder. We struggle to prioritise actions that will benefit our future self rather than what we want *right now*. This leads us to develop poor spending habits. You choose to do something that's easy over something that you know is better for your long-term money success.

One of my bad spending habits used to be ordering dinner through a food delivery app. I often couldn't be bothered to stop at the supermarket on the way home from work to pick up something to cook for dinner, so I'd go home and order in. I enjoyed the tasty food, and it was so easy—all done with a few flicks of my thumb and seven steps from my couch to my door to collect the food. Before I knew it, the habit was established.

But the result was that I was struggling to stick to my weekly budget. There was less money left over for the other things I wanted to do, specifically building my travel fund and savings account.

It took some conscious decisions and careful planning, but ultimately I decided things needed to change. For the next couple of years I worked hard on shifting my day-to-day money habits and behaviours in a way that made it easier for me to save and work to my budget and spending plan.

In the early days it was a real struggle, and I'd fairly frequently get off track, but over time I shifted my lifestyle and the spending behaviour that came with it. Instead of ordering in every night, I'd set aside time for shopping and food prep. Four coffees a day became two, then to relying on the Nespresso machine in the office. I've since gone back to café coffee but I'm now down to one a day. And instead of catching an Uber to every destination I prepare and walk more.

None of these things drastically reduced my quality of life, but they made a big difference to my ability to save. Today I find it easy to work within my spending plan, and I now allocate more money to travel and the bigger ticket things I get more real enjoyment from.

Changing your spending habits takes focus and effort, but it doesn't reduce the quality of your life, and the impact and financial opportunity are huge.

The juggle

These days it's easy to find yourself with a heap of different bank accounts, and to get caught in the constant juggle, shifting money from one account to another, hoping like hell that at the end of the pay cycle you've hit your savings targets.

Most often you haven't, but the more accounts and processes you have in your banking, the harder it is to figure out where you went wrong.

If you want to be good at saving, you need to make your money management easy.

I'm a bit of a process nut, and I've found that setting up an automated money management system goes a long way to making saving easier. The more you need to do manually, the more you can get wrong. Automating as much as you can will increase your chances of success.

This is a challenge, but also an opportunity. By automating your savings success, you save a heap of time and accelerate your journey to replacing your salary through investing.

Finding balance

My definition of true money success is saving (and investing) at a rate you're happy with *while* living the lifestyle you want. It's important to get ahead with your money, but you also want to enjoy your life.

Finding that balance isn't easy, because we're naturally drawn to wanting more. If you spend more money you receive an immediate pleasure hit and more fun and enjoyment today, but you'll save less.

You'll have more stuff, nicer things and experiences, a bigger house in a nicer suburb, more travel and more shiny toys to play with today. But you'll end up trapped, working forever, a slave to your pay cheque.

When you save too much, you'll make rapid progress and you'll replace your salary much faster. But when you achieve your goal, you'll likely look back and regret wasting those lean years you could have been enjoying more.

Balance is key. It's also not easy to find.

A great savings plan is one that has you saving at a rate you're happy with. Saving more or saving less will increase or decrease your rate of progress. To find your ideal savings number, consider the impact of different saving rates both today and into the future.

I'll cover this in detail later in the book when we build your money game plan, but for now aim for a starting savings number you feel good about.

What a budget isn't

There's a lot of fear and myths around budgeting that often create barriers that can stop you from getting started. And even once you've started they can stop you from following through.

A good budget doesn't mean you have to count every dollar you earn. It doesn't mean you can't live a good lifestyle. And it doesn't mean you need to spend less on anything that's *actually* important to you.

Good budgeting is simply about prioritisation. We all have priorities in relation to our day-to-day spending (and lifestyle), travel, where we live, how much we save and invest, what conveniences we choose to pay for ... the list goes on. Everyone's priorities are different. Travel is important for some, less so for others. Some prioritise living in a nice house or in an expensive area or suburb. Others love eating out regularly.

Budgeting success just means you've prioritised the things you most want to spend on while saving at a rate you're happy with. Getting there often requires you to deprioritise the things that are less important.

Importance of a system

But budgeting is only half the battle. I think almost everyone (myself included) has created a budget that didn't work.

When I started out in financial planning, I worked for a traditional money management company, where a lot of clients already had a heap of money and were close to retirement.

When I left that company, I moved to a small business that worked mostly with people who were in the early stages of their money and wealth-building journey. I helped people build out their financial plans. We mapped out the current position of their income, expenses, assets and liabilities, then used some financial planning tools to do scenario planning. We'd compare what it would look like if they bought shares or bought an investment property or bought their own home, or even did all three.

When we were creating these financial models, they looked good. I could see that in a reasonably short space of time my clients would create some solid money momentum, which in turn would open up a lot of other possibilities for them. They were excited, thinking about all the things they could achieve. I was excited, thinking about the next stage of their money journey and all the options I could help them take advantage of.

But then a funny thing happened.

When my clients checked in with me a few months later, almost all of them were off track. They hadn't saved as much as they had planned to. They hadn't invested as much as they'd planned to. And they hadn't made as much progress paying down their mortgages as they'd planned to.

They were disappointed. I was disappointed too.

Why most money goals fail

To figure out where things had gone wrong, we went back to the plan to make sure all our inputs were right (they were) and our assumptions were correct (they were) and that we'd not been too optimistic in our expectations (we hadn't).

When it came down to it, I discovered, the common denominator that was leading them astray was their savings rate. They hadn't hit their savings numbers, and this had a flow-on impact on everything else in the plan. All my clients had good, plausible reasons why things had played out the way they did and were confident the past few months were an anomaly — next time we spoke things would be back on track.

Sadly, again this didn't happen.

When I did my next round of check-ins with my clients, again things had cropped up that meant they didn't hit their savings targets, so *again* they were off track. Saving money is tough. Thinking it through, I realised that most of these people had never really developed a good savings muscle.

As a process nut, I figured that to be able to help my clients in the best way possible, I had to create a savings system that made it easier for them to hit their savings targets.

For the next four years I tested, measured, tweaked, refined and iterated a savings system that worked consistently across a broad group of diverse clients, significantly increasing their savings rates and outcomes. This is the savings system I've unpacked in this chapter.

Nailing your fail-safe savings system

Without a good savings system, you'll plan and get all pumped up to get the results you've planned for, but it's easy for life to get in the way. Something comes up in the month and you chalk it up as a one-off. But then it happens again. And again. And again. Before you know it, a heap of months have passed and you're nowhere near where you intended to be. This can be frustrating and stressful, and it kills your motivation.

From there it's easy to fall back into the trap of your old bad habits, burying your head in the sand and putting off your money success for that magical ideal tomorrow that never seems to come around.

On the flip side, when you nail your saving, spending and money management, your progress becomes so much easier. You get better results in less time and with less effort. And with less stress and more peace of mind, your confidence grows.

But first you have to get there.

Once you have a good savings *plan*, you need a good savings *system* to make it easier to get the results you're looking for. When you get this right, you can streamline your money management, automate your banking, save yourself a bunch of time and massively increase your chances of saving success.

Build the last budget you'll ever need

Creating a budget is something most people try at some point on their financial journey. But here's the thing: a budget on its own is close to useless, and in some cases can do more harm than good.

A budget is simply a tool to help you plan, save and manage your money better. It is a starting point, not the outcome you're after. The result you're looking for when you budget is to increase your savings number and get clearer on what money you have available that you can do something smart with.

I see budgeting and saving as activities that should always go hand in hand if you want your awesome savings *plans* to turn into *outcomes*.

To completely nail it with your savings and budget, there are some key steps you need to work through:

1. **Lay out your spending.** Look at what you have coming in and going out to find a savings rate you're happy with.
2. **Prioritise.** Determine the things that bring you real happiness and deprioritise everything else so you can save more.
3. **Think ahead.** Look at what will change and make sure any essential spending is provided for.
4. **Segregate and automate.** Structure your banking to automate your savings success.

I'll take you through these steps in detail, but to contextualise what you'll be working towards in this chapter I'll outline the savings system you'll build, as illustrated in figure 2.1.

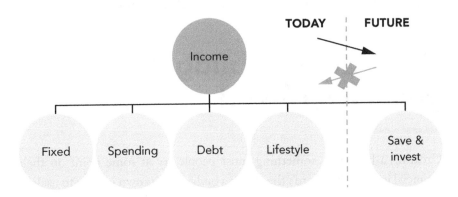

Figure 2.1 The Pivot automated saving system

The idea with this system is to have all your income coming into one central bank account, then filtering it into different buckets so you have the right money in the right place at the right time to nail your saving and spending plan.

When you're allocating your money, whether it's savings in a bank account or your regular income, you have only two choices. You can direct the money to your spending today or you can allocate it to your spending in the future.

Your future spending is your savings and investments. While saving in cash is important, it isn't going to make you rich—you need to invest. But pretty much all investments outside of cash can go up and down from year to year, so if you want to get good results when you invest you need to keep two things in mind. First, choose good investments (I'll cover that in the next couple of chapters). Second, never sell your good investments at the wrong time.

To ensure you're never forced to sell investments, make certain all the spending you want to do on the today side of things is provided for. This is a big part of the reason why having a rock-solid savings system is so important, and why it's important you take the time to get this right *before* you invest.

Now I'm going to take you through the steps to follow to build the last budget you'll ever need, and the system to make it *work*.

Step 1: Lay out your income and expenses

If you want to create a rock-solid saving and spending plan, the first thing you need to know is what money is coming in and what's going out. You can note these down on a piece of paper or in a spreadsheet, or you can access the savings planner template that you'll find with other book resources at pivotwealth.com.au/rsi/.

Reader tip: To understand the lay of the land and what's important when building your savings plan, first read this chapter to the end then loop back to work through this exercise.

As you're working through this process, know that the quality of your output is going to be driven by how much effort you put into it. Your savings plan is the foundation of your money strategy, so it's crucial to get it right. That said, you just need a starting point, so don't let getting it perfect stop you from getting it done.

As you're putting this together be conservative with your estimated inputs. Use numbers you're confident you can hit. Round down your income inputs and round up your expenses. This way when you put your plan into action, you're more likely to be pleasantly surprised than to be disappointed. If you underestimate your income or overestimate expenses, it's only going to mean you have more money left over. If you overestimate income or underestimate expenses, though, you can find yourself scrambling to deal with a shortfall.

Income

Start by laying out all sources of regular income, using the amount after tax that comes into your bank account.

In the irregular income section, list any other, less predictable sources of income, such as overtime, commission payments, bonus income and that crisp pineapple you got from Nana at Christmas.

Expenses

You have only so many types of expenses, including:

* fixed costs — your rent, bills, the boring-but-important stuff
* spending — your pocket money to cover food and entertainment and other day-to-day discretionary spending
* debt — to cover any mortgage payments or personal debt
* lifestyle — your big-ticket discretionary spending, such as travel
* savings (and investments) — the money you'll direct to replacing your salary by investing.

One of the common sticking points when doing a budget is focusing too much on how much you've spent in the past.

The past can be helpful when making sure you've set realistic expectations for the future, but outside of that it's largely irrelevant. This means you don't need to spend a heap of time trawling through your old bank statements to figure out where your money has gone (table 2.1). Instead, focus on what you want to spend in the year ahead.

Table 2.1 Spending and savings planning

Expense	Category	Amount ($)	Frequency
Regular income	Income	1300	weekly
Overtime	Income	150	weekly
Total income		**1450**	**weekly**
Rent	Fixed	500	weekly
Utilities		65	weekly
Subscriptions		40	weekly
Food shopping		220	weekly
Eating out		50	weekly
Holidays		150	weekly
Add new			
Add new			
Total expenses		**1025**	**weekly**
Net savings		**425**	**weekly**

As you're working through the savings and spending plan template, you'll notice there are heaps of different categories. Don't let this put you off; you probably won't have anything listed next to most of them. The long list is there as a prompt so you don't miss anything important.

As you're setting out your spending, keep in mind that later you'll circle back and prioritise, so these numbers will likely change. Don't get too caught up in making it perfect on your first pass.

Fixed expenses

These are your rent, bills and other boring (but important) spending. They're easy to predict and easy to automate, and once you've decided a fixed expense is important, it just needs to be paid without your giving it much thought. These expenses should be easy to find, as most of them will be coming out of your bank account or credit card regularly.

Debt

This one is everyone's least favourite category, but it's an important one. I'm not afraid of debt, and good debt is likely to be an important part of your money strategy (it's covered in detail later).

Bad debt drains your cashflow and savings capacity. Trying to get ahead with your money while running bad debt is like carrying water in a leaking bucket. It's two steps forward and one step back. It drives up your stress and reduces your feelings of money wellbeing.

A key step on your journey to money success and replacing your salary through investing is to eliminate bad debt from your life.

When you're listing your debts, start by including only your current minimum debt repayments. This isn't the strategy you're going to follow, but using the minimum repayments is important to give you a clear picture of how much money you actually have available to work with.

Ditching your (bad) debt for good

If you have personal debt, the first step is to make sure you're not paying more in interest costs than you need to. Reducing your interest costs will mean more of your repayments are reducing your debt instead of just covering dead interest expenses. Use a comparison site such as Finder.com.au to shop around and get the best deal.

Consolidating debts

If you have multiple debts, consider using a balance transfer credit card or consolidating your debt into one loan with a lower interest rate. If you go down this path, it is *absolutely critical* that you avoid the debt trap.

This happens when you use a balance transfer or consolidation loan and then continue to spend on your old credit, creating even more debt. If you consolidate debts, cut up any cards immediately *and* call up the provider and close down your credit account to eliminate any risk.

If you have a bad credit history, this may not be an option in the short term, and that's totally okay. It just means you need to move to the next step and play the waiting game until you can. Once your interest costs are reduced, it's time to attack your debts and ditch them for good.

Cascading debt repayments

If you have multiple debts, it can feel like you're not making any real progress on reducing them.

The most common strategy for paying down multiple debts is to spread your payments over each debt to gradually reduce them over time. The problem with this approach is that it's slow going.

An alternative is cascading debt repayments, a strategy I'm a big fan of. It works like this. First, you need to include your minimum repayments for all debts in your spending plan, and to make sure payments happen every month or week without fail.

Then, you take the amount of surplus you have available to you—for example, it might be $150 per week. Instead of spreading this amount over multiple debts, you target one specific debt you want to tackle first. It could be the debt with the highest interest rate, or it could be your smallest debt.

Paying down your high interest rate debt first is clearly best from an interest-saving perspective. But if you have a small debt at a lower rate, you might benefit from getting rid of this debt first to increase the amount of surplus you can apply to your other debts.

Once your first debt target has been eliminated, choose your next one and direct your repayments to it. Once that debt is gone, it's another minimum repayment eliminated that will increase your savings number, giving you more money to tackle your next debt target.

Rinse and repeat until you're debt free!

Spending

This is your main day-to-day discretionary spending, and it's the category that's responsible for most overspending. In addition to your general discretionary spending areas, such as entertainment, eating out and clothes, this category includes food and medical costs, two essential expenses.

Personally, looking after my health and the health of my family is a discretionary cost I see as crucial. But how much you spend on food and how much you spend on medical costs involves choices, which is why they're included in this category. Some other savings systems include these costs in the 'fixed' account bucket, but I think this is a mistake — mainly because the costs are in some cases necessary and this approach can lead to your spending the money you need for upcoming bills and then falling short.

Spending is also a category where unplanned costs can crop up irregularly. When this happens, if you want your savings plan to work you need to balance these expenses against your other spending. Given the expenses in this category are largely discretionary, this is the easiest place to find money that's not already allocated somewhere else.

How much money you allocate to this category is going to be a big driver of your day-to-day lifestyle. Make sure anything important is included, then ruthlessly cut out the rest so you can save more.

Lifestyle expenses

I should call out that the 'lifestyle' label here can be a little confusing. This category is for your bigger ticket, discretionary expenses and not necessarily for all expenses that contribute to your lifestyle.

This account isn't for brunch out with your mates on the weekend, but for those larger costs that are important to you but aren't provided for in your everyday spending allocation.

Without a good savings system it's common to spend more day to day and not put money aside for these expenses. If this happens, you either sacrifice or spend from savings (or, worse, on credit) to cover these costs, and you'll have to play catch-up afterwards.

This is my favourite category, because it's your bigger ticket spending on things like travel, experiences, new tech toys and things for your house. These expenses are the ones that bring you real enjoyment, so they're crucial to a spending plan you'll love.

Unexpected expenses

As part of your allocation to lifestyle spending you should include an allowance for unexpected expenses. You don't yet know what you'll need to spend this money on, but it may include things like having to replace your phone or some other piece of tech, or fixing something around the house.

Failing to include an allowance for these unexpected costs (and they will happen) will throw out your spending and saving plan and leave you scrambling to reallocate money from somewhere else. If this happens at the wrong time (which it often will), you can be caught short.

How much is right here depends on you and your spending and lifestyle. As a starting point, I suggest including between $1000 and $5000 annually. If you're not sure (and if your budget allows), you can start a little higher. If you don't need the money, you can always reduce your allocation or put the money back into savings and investments.

Step 2: Prioritise

You are in complete control of every aspect of your spending and saving plan. Your budget is simply a picture of what you're doing today. If you don't like the picture, you have the power to change it. Every element of your spending plan is within your control. No matter where you're at today, you should think of your budget and spending plan not as an outcome but as a starting point.

If you're like most people, when you include all your ideal spending over the next 12 months you're probably not saving as much as you want to. You may even end up in the red—I know that was the case for me the first time I went through this process.

This step is all about prioritising to get you to a point where you're happy with how much you're spending *and* how much money you have available to save and invest.

Some changes are easy to make, and others will require more work, planning and time to realise, but they all can be changed *if* that change is important to you and your money success.

Some elements are 'fixed' in the short term—things like rent and bills, your income, or debt you're now determined to ditch for good. These commitments need to be met, which may mean some short-term discomfort (or even pain). But over time you can change all these things to create a spending and savings plan that delivers the lifestyle and savings results you want.

Short-term/immediate prioritisation

It's easy for expenses to creep into our lives that don't bring much real happiness, satisfaction or value. This happens because we often make our spending choices in the moment, and in the moment our inner spender wants that pleasure hit that comes from spending.

You're always prioritising, and prioritising in the moment almost always leads you to choose priorities that aren't 100 per cent consistent with what's important to you.

The alternative: conscious prioritisation

You know you only have so much money to work with (at least for now). You know you want and need to save enough money to make the progress you want. And you know that spending outside your means will just result in your having to make sacrifices in other areas.

Longer term prioritisation

First, a warning: there's some serious potential and value in looking at how you can change your expenses and increase your income over time, but you should avoid relying on non-immediate changes to your income (or spending) to drive your savings success.

Avoid ending up in a situation where you're not saving much, or at all, but you have grand plans to change careers or move interstate to increase your savings capacity. It's easy for life to get in the way of such plans, and if you're deferring saving success until bigger changes are made you risk their taking longer than expected, and all the while you're financially 'treading water'.

Instead, create a savings plan where you're happy with how much you're saving tomorrow. Then if you change things over time that further increase your savings capacity, this will be the cream on top.

How to prioritise

Now it's time to assess. First, run through your expenses and look at each of them in turn, thinking through how important they are to you. While you're doing this, keep in mind that every dollar of expenses you eliminate is another dollar you'll have to save.

Everyone's priorities are different, so there's no one 'right way' or 'right amount' for you to save. The key is in making sure you're getting real happiness and value out of your spending.

As you're prioritising, your savings number will be constantly changing. Each time you make changes to your spending allocations, circle back to your savings number and see how it's tracking.

Getting to a position where you're happy with your spending and how much you're saving often takes a few rounds of prioritisation, so don't sweat it if you're not immediately exactly where you want to be. This just means you need to rinse and repeat. Doing this well can take a little time, but given your spending plan is going to dictate your everyday lifestyle, and your savings plan will dictate your rate of money progress, the juice is worth the squeeze here.

Before we jump into your prioritisation, I want to give you some motivation.

In Australia at the time of writing the average pre-tax income is $92 029 or $1342 per week after tax, and the average savings rate is 8.7 per cent, reflecting average weekly savings of $117.

If you could manage to double your savings rate to save an extra $117 per week and then invest that money into the share market, that money would grow over the next 10 years to be worth $102 675. Keep this going, and over 20, 30 and 40 years this extra savings would grow to be worth $375 162, $1 098 307 or $3 017 442.

Pretty powerful, right?

So now it's time to prioritise to pump your savings number.

Schooling and child-related costs

If you have kids, this might be a little controversial, but I can assure you there's merit in making deliberate spending choices for your children. Some parents push so hard to cover spending on kids that they're stressed out or are forced to make major sacrifices. In my opinion, it may sometimes be better to spend a bit less on your kids so your family can all enjoy life more.

If you don't yet have kids, READ THIS NOW. It will help you by planting some seeds that germinate and bear serious fruit later.

This is a category where I see a lot of people get things way out of whack. As a father of two gorgeous girls, I want the best for my kids. If there's something I think will add to their lives or happiness, I want to give it to them with all my heart. Fortunately for me, before having children I was lucky enough to benefit from the lessons learned by some of the people I've helped with their financial planning.

It's easy to go wrong with spending here by looking at each individual child-related spending decision in isolation. You ask yourself: Should my daughter have ballet lessons? Should my son play basketball? Should we send the kids to the more expensive school? Would my daughter enjoy horseback riding?

Positive answers to these questions often result in your making more commitments and spending more money, not to mention turning yourself into a never-ending taxi service. Before you know it you've committed to so many things that you're having to say no to other important things, or you're saving less, or both.

The alternative to the reactive approach of making these choices in the moment is to adopt a considered approach. Think through the things you could involve your kids in—private schooling, sporting activities, hobbies, travel, and all the things you think they might enjoy or value.

Then assess what these activities will cost and how they will fit with your other money goals. There's no one right way here. You'll know instinctively how important these things are to you.

Think through which activities come at low or no cost, and which ones are more expensive. This will help you assess what you think makes the most sense for your kids and your family while fitting in with your saving and investing goals.

Increasing your income

Controlling your spending is powerful and important, but there is a limit to how much you can cut your costs to increase your savings. There's no limit on how much you can increase your income, so it's important to keep this in mind if you want to maximise your financial potential.

Increasing your income can be managed in two ways. It can be done immediately by taking on more work, like getting a second job or working a gig economy job like driving Uber. The second and potentially more powerful way to increase your income is by accelerating or changing your career, potentially through upskilling or reskilling to work towards a significantly higher income.

All these approaches can work, but only you know whether and how they might work for you. Remember, again, that our aim here is for you to make conscious choices with your eyes open, having considered all the options. This way when you decide on your plan of attack you'll have total confidence it's the very best one for you.

Step 3: Think ahead

Once you've got your day-to-day spending sorted, you need to look at any big changes on the horizon. If there isn't anything significant here, this step is an easy one. But if there are changes coming up, you'll need to provide for them.

Think through any significant changes to your spending in the short term, things like major pay rises or income being reduced by time out of the workforce, or changes to childcare and schooling costs, rental or housing expenses, or an overseas relocation.

Your income and expenses are going to change in the months and years ahead, and an important part of staying on the front foot with your money is to review your planning regularly.

This means that at this point you don't need to worry too much about small, incremental changes. The only things you should be thinking through here are substantial changes that you know will have an impact on your rate of savings—things like taking time out of the workforce for the children, childcare and schooling costs, starting a business or changing careers.

This is particularly important when it comes to investing and making larger money moves like buying property, where you need to make sure your choices fit with your spending today and how this will change over time.

It's important to get clear on any larger one-off expenses you anticipate in the short term, like planning a wedding, maternity leave or travel, so these are provided for in your spending, saving and investing plan.

If you have enough cash savings, the easiest option here is to put this money aside immediately. This way you can start fresh with a plan that's going to be consistent with how you run things over the months and years ahead.

If you don't already have enough savings in place to cover these expenses, you'll need to allocate part of your regular savings to cover them. You can use the Moneysmart savings goals calculator (moneysmart.gov.au) to figure out exactly how much you need to save each week or month to have the money ready when you need it.

Step 4: Segregate and automate

At this point you should have a spending and savings *plan* you're happy with. Now you need to turn your savings *plan* into savings *results*. The aim of your savings system is:

- to make it easier for you to hit your savings targets
- to ensure you're never forced to sell investments at the wrong time
- to make your day-to-day money management easy
- to give you a feedback loop
- to help drive your motivation as you move forward.

How we get there is through your banking. I'm going to unpack the savings system I personally use, and one I've helped thousands of other people create to make their savings success easier.

There is a bit of detail here and work needed to make it happen, but I promise you the results are worth it. The good news is that you've already done most of the heavy lifting. Having laid out all your expenses in the savings planner, they are now grouped into categories that neatly line up with the accounts you'll set up for your banking.

Flip back to figure 2.1 earlier in the chapter for an illustration of the savings system we're going for. I'll unpack each of the accounts in turn.

Pro tip: When setting up your banking system, your savings plan or budget is your guide. If you're unsure about any expense and where it fits, refer back to the tool you've used to plan your savings and all will become clear.

Practical banking tips and hacks

This is where the rubber hits the road, so I want to unpack my top tips and the key things for you to focus on to make this work for you as easily as possible.

Where banking can go wrong

An important part of having a spending plan that works is balancing out your spending, particularly for your two discretionary buckets, spending and lifestyle costs. However carefully you predict your spending, unfortunately life tends not to respect nice neat spreadsheets (as much as that sometimes bothers me).

Reality is going to be different from your plan, and you need to be prepared for this. When life happens and unplanned expenses come up, you need to balance these against some of your other spending if you want your plan to work. This happens most commonly in your 'spending' and 'lifestyle' categories.

One week you may throw a party or buy a gift or go out for a nice meal, so you end up spending a little more. That then needs to be balanced against your other spending. Once your category spending allocations are set, it doesn't really matter what you spend your money on, so long as you don't spend more than you've allocated.

Choosing your banking providers

If you're running multiple bank accounts, you don't want regular fees and charges eating into your money. So to implement this system, you'll need to find a bank that offers fee-free bank accounts. You'll also need to choose a provider that gives you the right sort of access, such as card access and direct debit ability for your different buckets.

Thankfully there are a lot of good providers out there that offer this today. This is not financial advice or a recommendation, but I use a combination of Macquarie Bank, ING, and CBA for my personal banking and find this works well for me. But so long as the accounts are giving you what you want and need, use whatever providers you're most comfortable with.

Floating your accounts

When you set up this banking system, you will likely need to put some money into some (not all) of the different buckets as an account 'float'. This is most important for your bills and debt accounts, so things flow smoothly. It's possible in the first week of your savings cycle that the amount coming out of an account is more than you put into it because of monthly or quarterly bills or expenses. So if you start these accounts with zero dollars there's a risk your payments will bounce.

If, on the other hand, you were to open this account with, say, $10 000, so long as your planned expenses over the year are consistent with your actual expenses, in 12 months' time you should still have exactly $10k in your account.

Clearly, $10 000 is an unnecessarily large initial deposit, but it should help you determine the 'right' amount between $0 and $10k that will mean your accounts never run out of money. If you have the money available, you can start with a higher amount in your accounts and reduce it over time.

The offset account conspiracy

If you have a mortgage offset account, holding as much of your money as you can in this account will keep your interest costs as low as possible. But over the years I've found holding all your money in one bank account makes it close to impossible to achieve true savings success.

With all your money in one big pile, you lose clarity on how much you're saving. You feel like you have more money, so you spend more. And without clarity, planning well with your money goes out the window.

With the system I outline in the next section, your offset account can be used as your main savings account to hold your biggest bucket of cash. But I'm totally okay with holding some of your money in other bank accounts that won't save you as much in interest.

You may think this is a little crazy, but I can assure you that if you have an epic savings system that works, you'll save more than the interest savings from a mortgage offset.

Emergency savings

Having an emergency fund is important because it gives you a safety net. As an investor, having in place a solid emergency fund means you'll never be forced to sell your investments at a bad time.

There's no hard rule for the size of your emergency fund, because again this is driven by how you feel about your money, risk and your personal situation. If you're unsure about how much might be right for you, three months of your core living expenses would make a good starting point. Core expenses don't include your regular savings and lifestyle spending or some of your day-to-day expenses, as these expenses can be easily cut if needed.

Your banking buckets

I'll wind up this chapter by reviewing the five banking 'buckets' you'll need to sustain your savings plan.

Fixed

This account will most likely need a debit card attached to it. Note that this isn't the sort of debit card you should carry around in your pocket or digital wallet, because this account is only to cover your bills. Once you set up your account and link up all your bills, you should park the card at the back of your sock drawer—you won't need it again unless you choose to make changes.

The 'float' for this account needs some attention as bills can be lumpy, so take your time to get this right and it will save you a lot of time and frustration.

In this account, some of the expenses like your utilities will fluctuate from month to month, and that's okay. By being conservative with your estimates when you input these expenses in your savings planner will mean there's a little extra to cover higher than expected expenses, and your account floats will do the rest.

Spending

This is the account you'll use most days, so you'll want it to be easy to access, with a good app that lets you check in on your account balance while standing in line for your morning latte. I generally suggest using an account with the same bank you currently use for your day-to-day spending.

It's important this account is separate from your other bank accounts including your savings account. This helps create a small but effective barrier between you and getting off track. This alone won't guarantee your success, but it will help.

Debt

Having a stand-alone account for your debt repayments will give you flexibility about how you manage your debts moving forward and your good debt providers. It will also give you clarity on how much you're allocating to your debt repayments.

Not building your day-to-day banking around your current mortgage provider makes it much easier to switch mortgages and get the sharpest deal as often as you want or need to.

Lifestyle

In the early days of building your money muscle, having this account separate from your spending helps to keep it out of sight and out of mind.

Your lifestyle expenses typically aren't things that just 'come up' as you're walking down the street. They're bigger purchases, like booking a trip or buying yourself a new piece of tech. This means keeping the money separate from your day-to-day spending shouldn't create an issue.

Over time, as you create good money habits and behaviours, you can bring this account closer to your spending to make it more easily accessible.

Saving

Watching your savings grow is incredibly motivating, so it's important you keep this money in a separate bank account. It can be in a separate bank or with the same provider as your other non-spending bank accounts. If you have a mortgage with an offset account, this is often the best place to keep your chunky cash savings, as it will deliver you the highest rate of interest.

Following these steps will help you choose your banking providers and the accounts you want to use with them. From there you'll set up your banking buckets, float your accounts and automate your transfers between them.

I suggest using a weekly cadence for your transfers between accounts. This is most important for your spending account, where a weekly cadence means you're never more than seven days away from 'topping up' the account. This will help with your day-to-day planning and balancing out your spending over time.

THE WRAP

Your saving and spending dictate how quickly you get ahead, your lifestyle and what investing makes the most sense for you.

By now you should have created the last budget you'll ever need and a rock-solid spending and savings plan. And you'll have the system you need to turn your savings plans into results.

I totally get that there's a lot of meat in this chapter, but for good reason. It lays a strong foundation on which everything else that is to come as you work through this book is built, guaranteeing you get to the penthouse faster.

Your action plan

- [ ] Lay out your income and expenses to get clear on what money you have coming in, what's going out and what's left over.

- [ ] Prioritise what's most important to you and ruthlessly cut out the rest so you can save more.

- [ ] Think through how you might increase your income over time to save faster.

- [ ] Think ahead and plan around one-off expenses and bigger changes to your income and spending into the future.

- [ ] Choose your banking providers and the types of accounts you'll use with them.

- [ ] Open your bank accounts and 'float' them to get started.

- [ ] Redirect your salary into your hub account.

- [ ] Automate bills and debt repayments from your fixed and debt accounts.

- [ ] Set up your weekly transfer to automate your saving success.

CHAPTER 3

Invest to replace your salary

Investing is *the* key to not being forced to work forever. But if you're like most people, the fear of making a mistake is holding you back from reaching your true investing potential.

In this chapter, you'll learn how investing works, how you can build an income that is generated while you sleep without your lifting a finger, and how to get started.

First, I'm going to bust two common investing myths that drive investing fear and hold back so many people from investing success.

Myth #1: Risk is a bad thing.

When you invest, risk is actually what makes you money. It's also what can lose you money if you have the wrong risk or if you don't manage it well. Most investing risks can be managed but can't be eliminated altogether. When you invest, you're always accepting some risk; that's a good thing and exactly what you should be aiming for.

Myth #2: Choosing good investments is enough.

People focus so much on choosing good investments, they lose sight of the other important elements that go into being a successful investor.

To be a successful investor you need to do more than just choose good investments. You need to invest the right amount at the right time and to avoid selling investments at the wrong time. You need to be smart with your tax. You need to make sure your investments are working together as part of your broader money or wealth-building plan. And you need to keep yourself motivated and on track.

How much do you need to replace your salary by investing?

I want to start with an example showing how much you need to invest to replace the average salary in Australia ($92 029 as of May 2022). As noted in chapter 2, the rule of thumb when calculating how much you'll need in investments to replace this salary is to multiply this amount by 20 (or divide by 5 per cent). This gets us to $1 840 592.

Why do we use 5 per cent? This is based on the 30-year return of 9.8 per cent on the Australian share market. Assuming an allowance for fees and taxes of 2.3 per cent, and allowing for long-term inflation of 2.5 per cent, leaves you with a total return of 5 per cent to spend.

It gets a little technical but basically, allowing for taxes and fees as well as inflation, an investment portfolio of $1 840 592 today would deliver you an income of around $92 029 in the next 12 months. This income would then be indexed to inflation so you'd receive the same income in real, inflation-adjusted dollars every year for the rest of your life without eating into your original capital.

Note this is an approximation only, but it does give a good starting point for thinking about investing. Let's now go back to our example and how to build this level of wealth.

If you start with $0 in your investment account today, at age 20, and save and invest $10.10 daily, then reinvest all income (share dividends) over time, by the time you reach age 60 you'll have built total investments of $1 840 592.

If you start investing at age 30, you'll need to increase your daily investment to $27.72 to reach the same target. If you wait until age 40, your daily investment will need to be $81.11. And if you wait until age 50, you'll need to make a whopping daily investment of $296.38 to reach the same goal of $1 840 592.

This shows the power of time, but also the power of getting started.

Here's the thing. Most people know they should invest, but when it comes time to do so they stall. They worry about making a mistake, so it's easy to put it off for a tomorrow that never seems to come around.

If you fall into the inaction trap, you're missing out on the opportunity to start seriously building your money momentum, and you'll be forced to play catch-up later, saving and sacrificing more to get to the same result.

Underestimate long term, overestimate short term

You can see from this example that when you have time on your side you don't need to invest a lot of money to get some pretty epic outcomes. Einstein called compound interest the eighth wonder of the world, and in my opinion he was putting it mildly.

One thing I've noticed from helping people with their investing over the years is that we have a problem setting the right expectations around our investments. We have a tendency to overestimate how our investments should perform over the short term but underestimate how they should perform over the long term. This leads to a couple of serious issues.

When you overestimate what your investments should deliver for you in the short term, you essentially set unrealistically high expectations. Then, when your investments don't deliver the returns you were hoping for, it's easy to get frustrated and lose motivation. You then get distracted and drift off track. Ultimately you aren't consistent with your investing, so you don't build the momentum you should.

Underestimating how much your investments should do for you over the longer term also creates an issue.

Being crystal clear on how much momentum your investments can build over time leads to a huge boost in your motivation. So it's important you get clear on the long-term results you're heading towards. This motivation will drive you to get started, and to follow the path to investing success.

The solution is to set good expectations when you invest. This way you'll avoid short-term frustration and be more likely to follow through on your strategy, building your momentum.

To set your own investing expectations effectively, you'll want to use a compound interest calculator to look at how your investments are likely to grow based on how much money you're planning to invest.

When you do this, you'll see realistically how your investments are likely to grow over time. You'll probably be surprised by how much your investment growth starts accelerating over the long term if you stay consistent. You'll also notice that in the early years of your investment strategy the growth isn't earth-shatteringly fast.

Keep in mind that staying consistent in the earlier stages of your investment journey is *the* thing that drives the rapid acceleration in the later years.

Learn to be comfortable with 'slower' progress at the start so you can get rapid gains as you progress.

I unpack the steps for you to follow at the end of the chapter and there's a link to a calculator at pivotwealth.com.au/rsi/.

But setting realistic expectations in isolation won't give you the confidence to invest your life savings. To build this confidence, you need to understand investments, specifically investment risks and how they can be managed.

Growth vs defensive investments and your investment timeline

The first thing you need to understand about investments is the difference between growth investments and defensive investments (figure 3.1), and how much of each you should have in your portfolio.

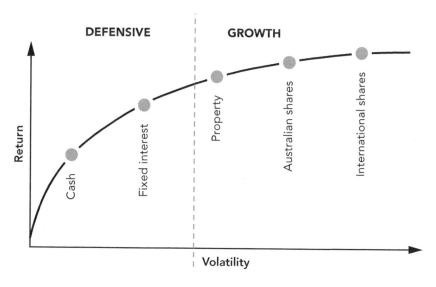

Figure 3.1 Defensive vs growth investments

The simplest example of a defensive investment is cash. Cash at the bank in Australia is government guaranteed up to $250 000 per bank, which means that even if the bank was to collapse you can't lose your money. Other defensive investments are term deposits, government and corporate bonds, and 'fixed income' investments.

It gets a little complex here, but these investments generally have more stability than growth investments such as shares because they're secured against assets, such as property.

Defensive investments are also referred to as 'income investments' because they're designed to generate an income, as opposed to investments such as shares that are designed to grow.

These investments, while relatively safe and stable, won't shoot the lights out from a return perspective. For example, the 30-year return on cash in Australia is 4.4 per cent, according to data from Canstar.

This brings us to growth investments, of which the most common are Australian shares, international shares, and residential and commercial property. These investments are designed to grow in value over time: you buy a share for $10 today and over time you hope it will increase in value.

With shares and other growth investments, you can expect them to go up over time, but they can go up and down on any given day. Your investment timeline is something important to understand, and importantly to ensure you're never forced to sell investments when markets are down (figure 3.2).

Your ideal mix of growth and defensive investments is largely driven by your investment timeline. The higher long-term return on growth investments means they're better for building wealth. But, because growth investments

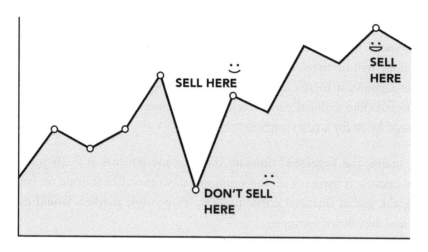

Figure 3.2 Share investments timeline

can go down (or up) by as much as 55 per cent in any given year, you need to make sure you're never forced to sell your investments at the wrong time. Table 3.1 shows the long-term returns on different types of investments.

Table 3.1 Long-term investment returns by investment type

Invest $10000 in 1992	Investment value in 2022 ($)	Per annum returns (%)
Australian shares	131413	9.8
US shares	182376	11.7
Australian-listed property	90243	9.3
International shares	94184	9.1
Australian bonds	55588	6.0
Cash	35758	4.4

When you have a shorter investment timeline, defensive investments are generally best because of the stability they provide. For example, if you know you're planning to buy a new car in six months and need $20k for the purchase, you could save the money in either a bank account or a share account.

If you save in a bank account, no matter what's going on in the world and financial markets, so long as you hit your savings targets you'll know the money will be there when you need it. But if you save the money in a share account, if there's a share market meltdown caused by something unexpected (like a global pandemic), when it comes time to buy your car you could be in for a nasty surprise.

With shares, the suggested timeline for your investments is 7–10 years. This is because if there is a serious economic downturn, like the one we saw during the global financial crisis in 2008, it's possible markets would go down and stay down for years.

If you invest in shares and need to 'cash out' during a market downturn, you'll be selling at a loss. Even if you sell in the early stages of a market recovery, it's unlikely you will receive a return close to the long-term average of 9.8 per cent.

Despite the suggested investment timeframe on shares of 7–10 years, it doesn't mean you should *want* or even *plan* to have the money invested for that long. It just means you should be prepared to leave it there that long if the market conditions suggest you should.

Perhaps you're looking to buy either your first property or your next property, saving up your deposit to make the property purchase happen. Property in Australia is generally expensive, so pulling together a deposit is no small undertaking. It often takes time to get there, and when you're saving money in a bank account it can be slow going and frustrating, especially when you consider the impact of inflation on the 'real' (inflation-adjusted) value of your money.

Because saving a deposit takes time and work, you need to keep yourself motivated and feel like you're making progress. It's common for people to start looking at how they can get this money working harder while they're saving.

Enter share investing.

But here's the thing. You might have crunched your numbers and figured out you'll have saved enough for your deposit in, say, 18 months, meaning you'll probably want to sell your shares and have the cash available.

Shares sound like a good idea, but if the markets are down, your deposit will be down too.

If you were to invest for the next 18 months and just before you want to buy your property there's a share market crash, it's not going to be a good idea to sell your shares. But if you don't *have* to buy your property (which you don't), you *can* leave the money invested until the markets recover.

In this case you probably also *could* invest more while markets are down, picking up more quality investments at a discount. Then all you need to do is wait for the markets to recover, and you'll likely gain much more than you were initially expecting.

This strategy would allow you to buy the same property with a bigger deposit and lower mortgage, or buy a more expensive property, or just have more money you can leave invested to grow your wealth.

The key element here is that you don't *need* the money—you just *want* it. If you're in this position, even if the timeline you'd like to work towards is shorter, shares can be a good option for investing.

And the odds are in your favour. Looking back over the past 20 years (2001–2021), on average Australian shares have gone backwards (lost money) in only four years out of 20. This suggests it's more likely shares will go up than down so you'll likely be able to buy your property when you want to. And you'll get to do so with the peace of mind that your money was working hard for you along the way.

But it's not without risk. If buying a property in 18 months is mission critical for you, then growth investments like shares probably aren't the right move.

The same applies if you have bigger upcoming expenses such as school fees, large travel expenses, a new car or home renovations. If these things *must* happen in a short timeline, then generally the best place to put the money is in defensive investments like your trusty old savings account. This way you know the money is safe and will be there when you need it.

Diversification

Diversification is a simple and effective way to manage and reduce risk when you invest. In figure 3.3 you can see how diversification can reduce the ups and downs of your investment portfolio.

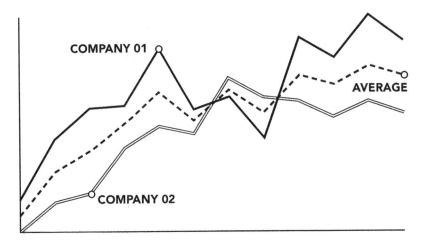

Figure 3.3 Diversification in practice

Consider this example. You invest $10 000 in Woolworths shares. The return on your investment is simply the return on the Woolworths shares. But if you were to 'diversify' your $10k by investing half in Woolworths and half in Commonwealth Bank shares, the return on your investment portfolio would be the average return across both companies. In investor jargon, you could say your portfolio was 'more diversified'.

At any point in time, one company would be performing better than the other, and this is likely to chop and change over time. But in your portfolio of the two investments, the highs of the best performing company will be balanced against the lows of the other. The result is that your overall investment return will be smoother.

This is a simple example with just two companies, but if you were to diversify your investing across 20 different companies, your returns would become even smoother.

It sounds obvious, but it's worth stating that the more investments you have in your portfolio, the less your total investment return depends on the return of any one individual investment or company.

When you have a highly diversified portfolio, you won't get that one big payday that can come if you pick a company that really takes off. On the flip side, you'll avoid the losses that come when you pick a dud company that goes bust or just slowly declines into nothingness.

Investing in 20 companies probably sounds like a lot of work, and it could be. Thankfully there are a heap of great investments available in the market today that give you 'instant diversification', where you buy one investment that holds a large number of different underlying shares, such as an ETF or managed investment fund. I'll cover these in detail shortly.

Small company vs big company risk

Most people who don't have a lot of investing experience (or any experience at all) think that when you start investing through 'high growth' investments, you start taking a lot of speculative risks.

Risk comes in layers, and not all shares are made equally.

Consider this example. Commonwealth Bank (CBA) is the second largest company in Australia. As of 31 August 2022, the total value of CBA was $166 billion. CBA is over 100 years old, has a proven track record of good performance, generates annual revenue in excess of $30 billion and has total assets of $1.22 trillion (yes, with a 't').

Because of its long track record, huge asset base, consistent revenue streams and diversified operations, I consider CBA to be a quality, stable, 'blue chip' investment. But it still falls under the banner of growth investments.

Now consider the smallest companies listed on the Australian stock exchange (ASX). I won't pick on any particular company, but the smallest listed companies start at a total value of just above $1 million. They're generally much younger companies. They don't have the same strong pool of assets behind them, and their revenue is much lower than big companies like CBA.

For these reasons, even though they are still considered growth investments, I look at these small companies as much higher risk investments. Typically, what happens with companies like this is that they get big and start performing strongly or they fail altogether or, most commonly, they plod along in mediocrity, eking out below-average returns over the long term.

So not all shares are made the same or experience the same volatility (figure 3.4). When you're investing, and particularly in the early stages of your wealth-building journey, avoiding smaller companies in your portfolio will go a long way to reducing the likelihood of your suffering serious setbacks and slow growth. If you focus on the big companies, you'll be better placed to get stable, consistent growth and avoid investment failure.

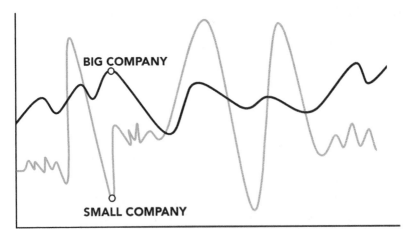

Figure 3.4 Small vs large company risk (volatility)

Investing in a high-growth or all-share portfolio does not mean you have to include more (or any) small companies in your investment portfolio. It simply means you have more shares like CBA, and fewer defensive investments like cash.

Active vs passive investing

Using the right investment approach will position you to achieve the best investing results in the shortest time. One key investor decision you need to make is on whether to follow an 'active' or 'passive' investment approach.

Active investing means, as the name suggests, your investments are managed actively — that is, you (or your investment fund or ETF manager) are choosing investments with the aim of doing better or differently than other investments. Figure 3.5 shows some typical active investing funds.

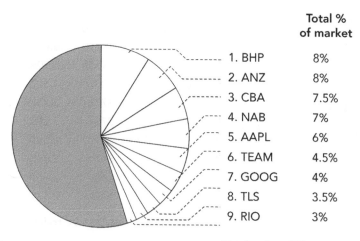

	Total % of market
1. BHP	8%
2. ANZ	8%
3. CBA	7.5%
4. NAB	7%
5. AAPL	6%
6. TEAM	4.5%
7. GOOG	4%
8. TLS	3.5%
9. RIO	3%

Total value: $5bn

Figure 3.5 Active investing funds

This normally involves a fund manager running calculations, trying to figure out which companies will perform best and choosing more of them, while avoiding companies they think will experience average performance or will go backwards.

But here's the thing: no one has a crystal ball, and even the experts often get their predictions wrong.

In contrast to active investing, passive investing means that instead of trying to pick the best performing investments, you're choosing to invest across the overall share market. A passive investment fund will buy up shares in every single company in a particular market in proportions relative to their size, so the return on the passive fund is the same as the return on the total market.

Passive investments are available for different markets, such as the Australian share market, US shares or international shares. Figures 3.6 and 3.7 show the combined value of the companies in Australian share market, and how an index fund mirrors the overall market.

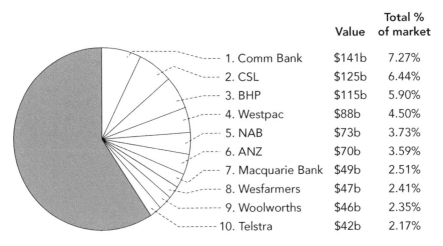

	Value	Total % of market
1. Comm Bank	$141b	7.27%
2. CSL	$125b	6.44%
3. BHP	$115b	5.90%
4. Westpac	$88b	4.50%
5. NAB	$73b	3.73%
6. ANZ	$70b	3.59%
7. Macquarie Bank	$49b	2.51%
8. Wesfarmers	$47b	2.41%
9. Woolworths	$46b	2.35%
10. Telstra	$42b	2.17%

Total value: AUD$1.94 trillion

Figure 3.6 ASX200 (top 200 Australian shares)

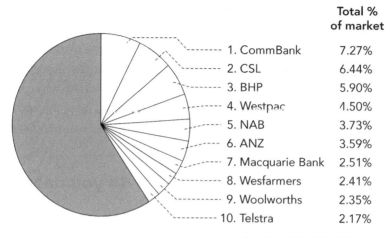

	Total % of market
1. CommBank	7.27%
2. CSL	6.44%
3. BHP	5.90%
4. Westpac	4.50%
5. NAB	3.73%
6. ANZ	3.59%
7. Macquarie Bank	2.51%
8. Wesfarmers	2.41%
9. Woolworths	2.35%
10. Telstra	2.17%

Total value: AUD$5 billion

Figure 3.7 Passive index investment funds

One of the things I like most about passive investments is that the only way they can really go bust is if every single company in the country was to go bust at the same time. If that were to happen, we're most likely talking about a zombie apocalypse or nuclear winter, and you'll likely have bigger problems to focus on than your investment returns.

Following a passive investing approach will mean your investments are highly diversified. It will also mean that you're seriously reducing any company-specific risk, and you can sleep like a baby at night knowing your investments are doing exactly what the market is doing.

Both active and passive investing have advantages and disadvantages. If you choose an amazing active investment fund, you can benefit from above-average returns. But on the flip side, if the active fund gets their decisions or assumptions wrong, you'll suffer through below-average returns.

The right choice for you is partly based on personal preference, and what you're trying to achieve as an investor. But it's worth noting that the statistics show that passive investments perform better than active investments over 95 per cent of the time.

In my view, when you invest what you're trying to access is the market returns. Anything above this is hard to consistently achieve, involves a lot of time and work (and expense), and carries more risk than the market. And given that we've seen in the example earlier in this chapter that investing just $10.10 per day can replace the Australian average salary, why put yourself through the hassle of trying to get more? You don't need the extra risk to get to where you want to be; you just need to avoid investment fails.

How much risk do you need?

You want your investments to make you as much money as possible. We've all heard the stories about investors who got into a company at the ground level and made a big pile of profit in a relatively short period of time.

But what you don't see is the risk that comes with this approach. If you're thinking about getting from where you are today to where you want to be with your money, your question shouldn't be 'How do I get there as quickly as possible?' if it means accepting significant risk of failure and having to go back to square one.

Instead, you should be asking yourself: 'How can I get to where I want to be with the most certainty possible?' This will shift the way you plan your investments and the investments you ultimately include in your portfolio.

You don't need to shoot the lights out with every investment you make, as we've seen from the examples unpacked in this chapter. But you do need to avoid setbacks and momentum-killing mistakes.

When advising my clients and for myself personally, I tend to favour a passive index investing approach. This removes almost all investment risk other than the risk of the market and your timeline risk. Your timeline risk can and should be managed with a rock-solid strategy and plan, and the market risk is exactly what you should be seeking out as an investor.

Active funds can be more useful for people who are close to or in retirement. In this case actively managing investments can increase investment income and reduce some of the market downside risk, two things that are valuable in the later stages of your investment journey.

Where investors go wrong: Selling at the wrong time

You only ever lose money on an investment when you sell.

So the more frequently you sell investments, the more potential opportunities you'll have to lose money. If you do a good job setting up your investment plan to begin with, you should only be buying investments you'll hold for the long term.

As time goes on, you may choose to sell down some good quality shares to do things like buy a property or pay down debt, but this will be the exception rather than the rule. To make this happen, you need to choose rock-solid investments you have total confidence in.

You and I both know that the share market will go down over time, but we also know that over the long term it will go up. It's never a fun time when your investments fall. But when you buy an index investment, if the market goes down, you're going to be less likely to freak out and sell at the wrong time, losing money as a result.

Ethical investing

Investments that fall under this banner are referred to by several different labels—ESG (environmental, social and governance), SRI (socially responsible investing), RI (responsible investing), impact investing, to name just a few. They all fall under the broader category of 'ethical investing', which essentially means investing that follows a set of values or ethical principles.

Ethical investing is an area worthy of its own book, so I'm only scratching the surface here. But given the increase in the number of ethical investment options and the talk around ethical investing, I want to explain the key things you need to know to establish whether ethical investing should be on your radar.

Essentially, ethical investing is about setting some guidelines around the sort of companies you will and won't invest in. The underlying principle is that you'll invest more in companies that are aligned with your values, and less with companies that aren't. This way companies that are aligned with your values have more investor support and can do more good work in their space, and those that aren't aligned have less investor support and expand less as a result.

The tricky part of ethical investing is that almost everyone's values are different. This means you may think a company or activity is 'ethical', while I may have a different view. For example, some people think all mining companies are unethical; others may think that rare earth mining is okay. Some may believe that only mining companies that have good social impact policies are worthy of investing in.

This creates challenges when choosing ethical investments, particularly if you're investing through a pooled investment option such as a managed fund, ETF or micro-investing.

Two main types of ethical investment funds are available: funds with 'negative screens' and funds with 'positive screens'. With a negative screen, companies are assessed relative to their peers to rate them on a number of environmental, social and governance factors. Companies that score poorly are 'screened out' and avoided when investing. With a positive screen, again companies are assessed relative to their peers and scored on various factors. The companies that score well are then included in an investment portfolio.

Do you need an adviser, banker or bank to invest?

The short answer is no. A financial adviser can and does help people set up investment accounts and invest money, but this is something you can absolutely do on your own, particularly if you're already confident around your choice of investments and how much you're going to invest. If you know exactly what you want to do with your investing and *only* need help to actually set up your investments, using an adviser is a more expensive path to a very similar outcome.

Where an adviser does add value is in helping you decide how you want to invest, what actual investments you want to use and how to invest in the most tax-effective way based on your situation. An adviser will also save you time by doing some of the heavy lifting around administration and setup for you. In Australia, the average cost of financial advice in 2022 was $3529 according to the Adviser Ratings Landscape Report, and using a high-impact, results-focused company will likely cost more. An adviser should of course add more value than the fee they charge you.

Any good advice firm will take on a client only when they know the client is going to end up ahead and be happy at the back end, so if you're not sure whether this is the right move for you it's worth speaking to several advisers to learn how their advice could help you.

If you're right at the start of your investing journey and have only a small amount of money to start with, you'll probably find that the cost of advice seems prohibitive. But if you're in the early stages of your investment journey and don't quite have the confidence to make it happen on your own, engaging an adviser can help you push through and take the action needed to build your momentum faster. The benefit of this will likely be measured in the tens or hundreds of thousands of dollars in the future, so don't let the thought of paying even a few thousand dollars for help lead you to get stuck in the inaction trap.

And if you're in a strong financial position, with more than a few thousand dollars and solid regular savings to start investing, you could shortcut your way to investing success by bringing an adviser into the picture sooner.

It's worth noting that ethical investments can be either passive or active. With passive ethical funds, an investment manager will typically start with a specific index such as the ASX200, then screen out companies that don't fit their investment criteria. With an active ethical fund or an impact fund, a fund manager will seek out companies they feel have a strong positive impact and include these in their investment portfolio.

Formulate your investment strategy

I've found that when you're making your money choices it's helpful to chunk down decisions into bite-size pieces. This way you only need to decide on the next step, which is easier than trying to figure out a dozen things at the same time.

Through the rest of this chapter, I'm going to cover the different types of investments you can use, including ETFs, managed funds and micro-investing. At this point you should have enough knowledge to be able to choose the investment approach you want to follow now and into the future.

Your key decisions are whether you want to follow a passive index investing strategy or an active strategy, and whether to take an ethical passive or ethical active approach. Each option has advantages and disadvantages, as discussed, so don't let trying to make it perfect stop you from getting this done. After working through the other decisions outlined in this chapter you'll arrive at a point where you're ready to take action.

Franking credits are your friend

In Australia, one of the more complex (and helpful) tax rules is around 'franking credits'. The term can be confusing, but as an investor it's important you understand franking credits and how they can help you. I'll dive deeper into this in the chapter on tax, but I'll set the scene here while we're talking about building your investment plan.

I'll illustrate it with an example. CBA earns a bunch of revenue, pays expenses and is left with a big pile of profit. CBA then pays corporate tax on the profits. Typically, they then reinvest part of the after-tax profit into growing the business and pay out part of the profit to shareholders through dividends.

When these dividends are received by shareholders, because tax has already been paid by CBA, there's a tax credit (or franking credit) attached to the dividend. This is reported back to the Australian Taxation Office (ATO) and included in your dividend statements. Then, when you do your tax return, the tax credit is applied to your tax return as if you're the one who paid the tax in the first place.

This means you pay less tax on dividend income when it's got franking credits attached than you would for any other investment income. Magic.

These franking credits make a big difference to your after-tax investment return and are one reason it's valuable to have Australian shares in your investment portfolio.

Types of investments

There are a few key options you can use when it comes to the types of investments available. You can buy 'direct shares' (individual shares), use a managed fund, jump on the exchange-traded fund (ETF) trend, invest through listed investment companies (LICs) or use a micro-investing app or platform.

Here I'll unpack the advantages and disadvantages of each, so you make the best choice for you.

Direct shares

Buying shares directly is the oldest and most traditional form of investing. This approach is also simple to understand. When you buy a share in a company, you're essentially buying a tiny slice of the company.

Because you own a small slice of the company, you're entitled to a small slice of the profits and increase of the value of the company. Any profits generated from the business activities are either reinvested in the company or paid out to shareholders in the form of dividends.

The big advantage of buying shares is that you can find one company you either believe in or think will perform well and invest in that company directly. If the company does well, your investments do well.

The main downside of direct share investing is the lack of diversification, because you're just buying into one company at a time instead of investing through something like an ETF or fund where you get immediate access to dozens (or hundreds) of companies.

It may seem obvious, but it's worth noting that when you buy shares directly you're essentially taking an 'active' investment approach. This is because you're making a choice around which companies you'll invest in and which you'll avoid. If you want to follow a passive approach, direct shares probably aren't for you.

Another downside of share investing is around investing costs. When you buy shares, you'll generally pay a 'brokerage' fee to the broker or online brokerage platform you use to do your investing. These fees can range from $5 to $30 per 'trade' (parcel of shares) you make. If you're buying shares in multiple companies to build a portfolio, these costs can really add up and drag on your investment return.

Managed funds

In a managed fund your money is pooled with that of other investors and invested by a professional fund manager. The fund manager will invest the money in investments such as shares, with the gains (and, potentially, the losses) spread across all the investors in the pool.

Through a managed fund you get exposure to a large number of shares, giving you 'instant diversification'. Because you're part of a large pool of investors that together are investing significant amounts of money, costs are lower, as you're getting wholesale access to investment markets and trading.

There is also a wide range of different types of managed funds available, some passive, some active, others ethical or socially responsible. Whatever your investment philosophy, there's likely a heap of different managed funds that can deliver your preferred approach.

The costs of managed funds can also be lower, particularly if you're investing regularly. Managed funds typically don't charge any transaction or entry fees, so if you're investing small regular amounts this can be more cost effective than some of the other options out there.

One downside of managed funds is around tax. The details here get pretty complicated pretty quickly, but the high-level version is that because you're in a pool with other investors the tax outcomes are shared. As other investors inside your managed fund are selling investments, any tax consequences are spread across all investors. This means you could be paying capital gains tax even on an investment you're holding for the long term simply because other investors are selling.

Exchange-traded funds

An exchange-traded fund (ETF) is another pooled investment, similar to a managed fund but with a couple of key differences. ETFs are bought and sold on the stock exchange in the same way you'd buy and sell shares.

ETFs have become wildly popular in recent years, and for good reason. There are a wide range of ETFs available that can give you access to everything from passive index investments, active investments and ethical investments to more exotic options like cryptocurrency and gold.

One advantage of ETFs is that, like managed funds, they provide instant diversification. You purchase one ETF and get immediate access to a large number of underlying investments.

Another advantage of ETFs is they offer more control over tax outcomes. Again, it gets complex, but essentially with most ETFs you're buying small slices of individual shares, so if you hold your ETF for the long term you don't incur capital gains tax unless your shares are actually sold.

One downside of ETFs is that they typically entail transaction costs, meaning each time you purchase an ETF you need to pay a brokerage fee. If you're investing small amounts regularly, this regular cost can slow down the growth of your investment portfolio.

Listed investment companies

Listed investment companies (LICs) are less common and are declining in popularity through the rise of access to quality investments such as managed funds and ETFs at a low cost, but in the interest of completeness I include them here. A listed investment company is a company that's listed on the stock exchange that is set up just to invest, generally in shares.

The advantage of LICs is that they give you instant diversification, typically pay good dividends and spread investing expenses across a large number of investors.

One downside of LICs is again a little technical, but if the company isn't managed well, the value of your LIC share can fall below the value of the underlying investments.

In my opinion, while LICs can do well there are better ways to invest. For the reason given, I personally avoid including these in my investment portfolio. LIC's aren't *bad*, but there are better options.

Micro-investing

Micro-investing is relatively new to the Australian investor landscape, but it has exploded onto the scene in a big way.

Micro-investing players generally offer a pretty slick user experience, giving investors easy access to fractions of underlying shares, ETFs or managed funds (or all three). The big advantage of micro-investing is you can invest very small amounts of money (as little as one cent).

Because you can start with very small amounts, these apps are a great place to get started. You can choose from a heap of underlying investments and gain instant diversification at a low cost.

Historically, micro-investing was the place for new investors to get started and wasn't as competitive an offering for more established investors. But as the costs of micro-investing platforms have come down and the range of micro-investing options has increased, these platforms have become worth considering even by serious investors.

Choosing between the options

You should now have a good understanding of your investing options. I totally get that choosing between them can feel overwhelming. But here's the thing: while each of these different types of investments and platforms has distinguishing features, the impact in actual dollars is small. The costs are broadly similar across the options. Access to investments is similar, as are the tax consequences.

The exception here is shares, which are not pooled. But given that most investors choose pooled investments over direct shares I'll focus my discussion there.

This might be a little controversial for my buddies in personal finance, but what this really means for you is that it doesn't *actually* make that much difference whether you choose to use an ETF, managed fund or micro-investing platform—particularly in the early days of your wealth building.

Once you get to $100k in investments I think it makes sense to take a solid stocktake of your options and make sure you're in the right place. But even then there probably isn't that much to choose between them. It's only really when you get into the several hundreds of thousands of dollars that you'll notice any real difference to your bottom line returns from one option over another.

APRA and ASIC protections

Another thing you should know at this point is that all mainstream investment options in Australia are regulated by the Australian Securities and Investments Commission (ASIC) and the Australian Prudential Regulatory Authority (APRA). The main role of these federal regulators is to protect investors, and they do a very good job of it.

There's a heap of complexity around this that I won't go into here, but you should know that it doesn't matter which investment product or company you use, so long as the product or platform has a financial services guide and a product disclosure statement, you have the benefit of the protection afforded to retail clients under the law.

Under ASIC's protections, the companies are required to have in place investor protection mechanisms. All investor money must be kept separate from the company's operational funds, so If a company were to go out of business tomorrow, investors' funds would not be put at risk. Investors would simply need to find another provider to run their administration and reporting (and to collect and cash their dividend cheques). ASIC also ensures that these companies meet their licensee and responsible entity obligations.

So if there isn't a significant difference between the options and they're all fully protected by APRA, instead of spending a heap of time on which investment account is best, you can focus on which type of investment is aligned with how you want to invest. Look for an investment account that gives you access to the style of investments you want, and that's easy to open, easy to use and easy to automate your regular investments.

If you're new to investing, micro-investing is probably the easiest place to start. These platforms have a slick user experience, and you can set up an account on your smartphone and start investing immediately.

If you're looking to choose a micro-investing account, I suggest looking at a few and even opening multiple accounts and putting a few bucks into each to see how easy it is and how you find the system. Look at costs, though the costs of most platforms are pretty similar. For me this means that to choose a platform you should be looking at which one you like the most and find easiest to use.

If you're a little further along, or if you want to have more input and control over your investments, using ETFs through an online broker is worth looking into. Managed funds are solid for all investors; the real downside is the admin that comes with setting up and running a managed fund account.

The following are platforms to consider.

Micro-investing:

- Raiz
- Pearler
- Sharesies
- Superhero
- Stake

Direct shares and ETFS:

- CommSec and CommSec pocket
- Pearler
- Selfwealth
- Etrade
- Sharesies

Managed funds:

- Vanguard
- Blackrock
- Russell

How much should you invest

You should now be clear on what sort of investment strategy you're going to follow, and you should understand and have some idea of what sort of investment account you're going to use. Now comes the all-important question of how much you should invest.

This is a decision many people agonise over, allowing it to become a roadblock to getting started. Fall into this trap and you'll be missing out on the opportunity to start building your investing momentum.

A word of (general) advice: The important thing here is that you just get started. It doesn't matter how small your initial investment is. As I've noted, you can start by investing as little as one cent! The more you invest, the faster your investments will grow. But if you're new to investing or just super nervous when it comes to your money decisions, starting small is totally okay, and a thousand times better than doing nothing.

If you've been investing for a little while already, or if you've done enough research to confidently take some bigger steps into investing, great. I suggest that when you're deciding how much to invest, whether that's cash you've already saved in a dedicated bank account, or your regular savings from your income, or both, you only invest money you're prepared to leave invested for years if the share market starts to crash.

From chapter 2, on saving, you should be clear on what money you need for your spending, and a crucial part of investing is making sure you don't need to 'dip into' your investments to cover any upcoming costs. You should also have an emergency fund in place to protect you against the unexpected. Any other money you have is fair game for your investing.

When you invest, you should do so with the knowledge that the share market will go down at some point, and that the money you're putting in will likely need to stay invested for years. This way you're setting the right expectations. If market conditions are good, you make a bunch of money and you want to sell your share investments to use the money somewhere else, no problem.

But if the markets are down, you'll have already expected this to happen, so instead of freaking out and selling at a loss, you'll recognise this for the opportunity it is to invest more and get ahead faster.

Consistency is critical when you invest. Small investments made regularly will create epic results over time, but you have to be consistent. Many of the platforms mentioned in this chapter have a feature allowing you to set up a regular recurring investment from any bank account, having money taken out and invested weekly or even daily.

The right frequency depends on your situation and how much you're investing, but I like the weekly cadence. In the past I've even done daily investing, having money debited out of my pocket money account, and I found that I hardly even noticed the money coming out.

You can also invest monthly or less regularly, but to keep you focused on your investing I generally recommend either weekly or daily investing as the best place to start. This way you'll see your investments growing regularly, you'll be more likely to look at how they're going, and as a result you'll build your knowledge and understanding of investments faster.

My challenge to you is to *get started today*. Investing is a skill, a behaviour, a habit, a muscle you build over time. The sooner you get started, the sooner you start flexing the muscle and building your knowledge and confidence around investing.

I hear you: *Things are tight right now and I just don't have enough to spare.* But, please forgive me for saying this, you and I both know that's BS. You can get started with as little as a single cent, and I guarantee you that if you do, you'll start building an interest around investing that will motivate you to do more. Before you know it, you'll be upping your investments, and making progress towards replacing your salary through investing.

You may also be in a position where you're saving hard for something big—maybe your first property, a wedding or taking time out of the workforce to start a family. Perhaps you want to build your cash savings to provide for this upcoming spending or investment. That makes a lot of sense, but again you can still do *some* level of investing. It doesn't have to be huge, just something.

Start with a small initial investment and set up a small regular investment plan with, at minimum, weekly contributions. Your future self will thank you for it.

And *boom*, you're an investor. Don't worry too much about becoming an investment expert at the start. As soon as you begin investing, you'll start learning. You'll see what's going on in the markets. You'll start lining up what's going on in the headlines with what's going on with your investments. And you'll start building your investing confidence.

THE WRAP

Investing is the key to not being forced to work forever. How much you invest and what investments you choose will dictate how quickly you replace your salary by investing. This is an area you have to get right, and the sooner you get your investments on track the easier everything else becomes.

Fear of making a mistake is the one thing that stands between you and getting the investment results you want and need. This fear can be overcome by building your knowledge, but also by building confidence over time as you take action investing.

Once you get started investing, you'll immediately start learning. You'll pick things up along the way, and at the same time your confidence will grow. Before you know it, you'll be an investment pro reaping the rewards.

There's a lot of noise around the investing space, and there are a lot of players who make investing out to be more complicated than it is. Simple is effective; boring is profitable. Any investor can build the knowledge and skills to achieve success here...

But no one will do it for you—you have to make it happen.

Your action steps

I know we've covered a lot of ground in this chapter. I've broken it down into 10 clear action steps you need to take to get started investing:

1. Study the risks section of this chapter until you're clear on the key investment risks and comfortable with how you'll manage them.

2. Use a compound interest calculator to set your investment goals and expectations.

3. Choose how much money you'll invest in shares versus how much you'll keep in cash.

4. Choose your investment style—active, passive, ethical active or ethical passive.

5. Decide on the investments you want to use—micro, ETFs or managed funds.

6. Choose your preferred investment provider and open an account with them.

7. Select your investment option for any new contributions into the account.

8. If you're making an initial investment, transfer money in to get started!

9. Set up a regular direct deposit into your investment account.

10. Sit back and enjoy the journey to replace your salary by investing.

CHAPTER 4

Buy property like a pro

I'll cut to the chase—property is the fastest way to build wealth, and it's crucial you get it right if you are to come anywhere close to achieving your financial potential. It's possible to replace your salary by investing without property, but in my opinion if you ignore property you're leaving money on the table.

That said, buying property in Australia isn't easy, and it's an area that's full of risk. If your property risk isn't well managed, instead of being an accelerator of your wealth building it can seriously slow you down. But these risks can be managed, and in this chapter I'll show you how you can buy property the smart way to get ahead faster.

Property vs shares

When you look at the long-term expected returns of property, you might be surprised to learn that they are actually very close to the returns on shares.

Reviewing Westpac data going back 150 years, the long-term growth return of Australian property comes in at 6.3 per cent. But this is only part of the picture, because when you invest through property you receive part of your return from the growth in the value of property, and the rest in the income you receive in the form of rent.

According to the CoreLogic quarterly rental review in October 2022, the average income return on Australian property is 3.36 per cent. When you own a property you also need to account for ongoing property costs such as strata and rates, and an allowance for insurances and maintenance costs, which is on average 1 per cent. This brings the total long-term return (growth + income) to 8.66 per cent.

Looking at the long-term return on a share portfolio, as discussed in the previous chapter the 30-year return is 9.8 per cent. Now I hear what you're thinking: *Ben, you just said that property was better than shares, but the return on shares is higher — that doesn't make sense.*

You're right. The overall return on shares is higher. But here's the thing: when you buy property you don't save up $500000 and then go and buy a $500k property. You save up a much smaller amount as a deposit, then borrow the rest from the bank so you can go off and buy your property.

A typical property deposit is 20 per cent, so you put down 20 per cent in savings and borrow the rest. You add your 20 per cent to the bank's 80 per cent, and suddenly you're able to invest in a property that's worth five times as much as you've saved up in cash.

This is called 'leverage', and it's leverage that makes all the difference when you buy property.

The power of leverage

Table 4.1 illustrates this with some numbers.

Table 4.1 Returns on property vs shares

Year	1	2	3	4	5	10	20	30	40
Shares $100k @9.8%	$110252	$121556	$134018	$147758	$162907	$265387	$704304	$1869133	$4690442
Property $500k @6.3%	$532426	$566954	$603722	$642874	$684565	$937259	$1756910	$3293362	$6173469

There are a few things to point out from the figures above.

First, it's worth noting that this example assumes the long-term return is achieved consistently every single year. We know that won't be the case, because both the share market and the property market have highs and lows. Some years they'll perform well above the long-term return; other years they'll perform below it (or even go backwards). You should be prepared for variations from year to year.

Property wins

You can see that the long-term return on shares is strong, and that keeping money invested for a long time will create some serious results. But when you look at the total return on your property investment, you can see that even though the return percentage is lower, property is a clear winner. This is driven by the fact that you're starting with a much bigger initial investment, which then grows and compounds over the years ahead.

To keep things simple, I've included the growth return on property but excluded the rent, so the total return you'd get from your property investment is significantly higher than I've stated. Also—a callout for the engineers and teachers among you—this simple example doesn't include things like tax or borrowing costs.

Not including borrowing costs makes the property option look a little rosier than it is in reality. That said, you can see from these figures that given property is *so* much better than shares from a total return perspective, there's plenty of room to cover borrowing costs of 5 per cent, 6 per cent or even 7 per cent and still end up way better off.

Tax impact

When looking at taxes, this works to make share investing look better than it actually is. I'm going to dive deep into taxes later, but keeping it a high level for now there's a couple of things to note.

When you invest in shares and those shares pay income in the form of dividends, you pay tax on the dividends in the year they are received. The tax isn't huge, but it also isn't insignificant, so the total returns after tax would be lower than was shown in the previous example. When you invest in property, you receive tax deductions that reduce your overall tax bill, so the total property return figures included are understated.

You can see from these figures that share investing is powerful and will put you on a clear path to replacing your salary. You don't need property, and if you're really fearful of property or have a deep distrust of property, or are anti-property for any other reason, you can still take some serious steps towards ultimately replacing your salary by investing. But property will help you to get there faster.

Almost all the risks involved in buying property can be well managed with the right approach. So if property will get you there faster and easier, why wouldn't you use it?

And it gets even better. These numbers assume you use a cash deposit to buy your property. This is probably how you would go about buying your first property. But once you get into the property market, you can invest using the increase in the value of your property (equity) and buy property without the need for a cash deposit.

Investing with equity

There are very few 'free rides' when it comes to investing, but investing with equity is probably as close as you can get to one.

It's worth starting with the basics here. Property equity is simply the difference between the value of your property and how much you owe on your mortgage. For example, if your property is worth $500 000 and you owe $300k, your equity is $200k ($500k – $300k).

In Australia, the banks will comfortably lend you up to 80 per cent of the value of a property. You need to be able to service the mortgage—that is, have a stable income and buy a property that will give you enough rent to cover the ongoing mortgage and other costs. But, assuming you can cover the mortgage payments in the eyes of the bank, borrowing should be relatively straightforward.

So over time as your property increases in value, your equity value will increase. You can then borrow against this equity and use the money for further investing, such as buying another property or investing in shares.

How equity release works

There is a bit of complexity here, but it's also fairly simple when you know how it works. The short version is that as your property value and equity increase, the banks will be more comfortable about lending you more money against your equity.

You'll generally need to make a cash deposit when you buy your first property. But once you have property equity, the banks will lend you money against your equity that you can use as the deposit for your next property. This way you could buy your second and any subsequent properties without using a cash deposit or putting any of your own money down. You're essentially using the bank's money to invest, growing your assets and wealth faster. This is a big part of why I believe that property is *the* fastest track to wealth.

Returning to our example, table 4.2 shows how much money you could potentially borrow at any point as the value of your property increases over time.

Table 4.2 Borrowing with property equity

Year	1	2	3	4	5	10	20	30	40
Property $500k @6.3%	$531 500	$564 985	$600 579	$638 415	$678 635	$921 091	$1 696 818	$3 125 849	$5 758 384
Equity @80%	$425 200	$451 988	$480 463	$510 732	$542 908	$736 873	$1 357 455	$2 500 679	$4 606 707
Loan	$400 000	$400 000	$400 000	$400 000	$400 000	$400 000	$400 000	$400 000	$400 000
Borrowing available	$25 200	$51 988	$80 463	$110 732	$142 908	$336 873	$957 455	$2 100 679	$4 206 707

In the early days, the growth in your equity is slower because you're starting with a lower base, but you can see that as your momentum builds the year-on-year increases start accelerating.

Table 4.3 shows what this could look like with two properties, which you see has some serious wealth-building potential. Note that $500k is way below the Australian average property value of $928 812, and that we're only using two properties, so there is potential for your results to be even better than what's outlined here.

Table 4.3 Growing your assets with multiple properties

Year	1	2	3	4	5	10	20	30	40
Property 1 $500k @6.3%	$531500	$564985	$600579	$638415	$678635	$921091	$1696818	$3125849	$5758384
Equity @80%	$425200	$451988	$480463	$510732	$542908	$736873	$1357455	$2500679	$4606707
Loan	$400000	$400000	$400000	$400000	$400000	$400000	$400000	$400000	$400000
Borrowing available	$25200	$51988	$80463	$110732	$142908	$336873	$957455	$2100679	$4206707
Property 2 @$500k	$0	$0	$0	$500000	$531500	$721389	$1328930	$2448132	$4509906
Property 2 loan	$0	$0	$0	$500000	$500000	$500000	$500000	$500000	$50000
Property 2 equity	$0	$0	$0	$0	$31500	$221389	$828930	$1948132	$4009906
Total assets	$531500	$564985	$600579	$1138415	$1210135	$1642480	$3025749	$5573981	$10268290
Total debt	$400000	$400000	$400000	$900000	$900000	$900000	$900000	$900000	$900000
Total wealth (assets - debt)	$131500	$164985	$200579	$238415	$310135	$742480	$2125749	$4673981	$9368290

Family guarantee

I've outlined how equity release works to help you buy a property. The family guarantee works in the same way, with the one big difference that instead of using the equity in your property as a deposit, you use the equity in a family member's property.

It's natural to have fear around a family guarantee, and this stops many people from pursuing this as an option. But in reality the biggest risk is that you choose to not make your mortgage payments, which can be avoided with the right planning and risk management around your property purchase.

If your parents (or other family members) own a property with some equity and you think this might be possible for you, I'd strongly suggest seeking out a good professional to help you understand how a family guarantee could work for you.

This strategy is definitely not for everyone, but if it does work for you it's something that can help you buy your first property and get onto the property ladder faster.

You don't need 10 properties

You can see from these figures that buying property is a powerful way to grow your wealth. I also think it's a great investment.

You don't need a heap of properties. Table 4.4 shows how property would grow over time using our 150-year long-term growth rate of 6.3 per cent. For now, don't worry about how many properties or what type (I'll cover this later in the chapter), instead we'll focus on the total value of your property and how that's likely to grow over time.

Table 4.4 Property growth

Starting value	Year 1	Year 5	Year 10	Year 15	Year 20	Year 30	Year 40
$1 000 000	$1 063 000	$1 357 270	$1 842 182	$2 500 339	$3 393 636	$6 251 697	$11 516 767
$2 000 000	$2 126 000	$2 714 540	$3 684 365	$5 000 679	$6 787 273	$12 503 394	$23 033 534
$3 000 000	$3 189 000	$4 071 811	$5 526 547	$7 501 018	$10 180 909	$18 755 092	$34 550 301
$4 000 000	$4 252 000	$5 429 081	$7 368 730	$10 001 358	$13 574 545	$25 006 789	$46 067 068
$5 000 000	$5 315 000	$6 786 351	$9 210 912	$12 501 697	$16 968 181	$31 258 486	$57 583 835

You can see from this that starting with $1 million of investment property value, over 10 years you'd make a total of $842 182 after taking away your starting property value. Over 20, 30 and 40 years you'd be looking at growth of $2 393 636, $5 251 697, and $10 516 767, respectively.

If you have more property, the numbers get even bigger — and quickly. This tells me you don't need 10 properties. You probably don't even need five. But the more you have, the faster your wealth will grow.

On paper, the strategy that can get you from where you are today to replacing your salary fastest will be to borrow as much money as the banks will lend and buy as much property as possible, all as quickly as possible. But this is often not the best strategy for most people, because you need to manage your risk (and you need to be able to sleep at night).

How much does it cost to own an investment property?

Owning an investment property isn't nearly as expensive as most people think. The average annual cost of owning an investment property worth $1 million is $20305. Based on the long-term property growth rate of 6.3 per cent, the expected annual growth on a $1 million investment property should average around $63000.

The numbers stack up nicely here: if you're paying around $20k for a $63k benefit, you're ahead by more than $40k *every single year*.

Initial costs of buying a property

When you purchase a property you'll need to pay some initial costs such as stamp duty, building and pest inspections, and legal costs. These costs on average equate to around 5 per cent of the property value, which on a $1 million property means $50000 in initial purchase costs.

Ongoing costs of owning a property

When you own an investment property you have to pay ongoing costs such as strata fees for apartments and townhouses, council rates for houses, water rates, insurance, property management fees, and repairs and maintenance costs.

These costs tend to average out at around 1 per cent of the property value, so for a $1 million property you'll face around $10000 each year in ongoing costs.

Then you've got your mortgage interest costs. According to data from Finder.com.au, in November 2022 the average variable mortgage interest rate in Australia was 5.20 per cent. Based on a 30-year mortgage of $1 050 000 (purchase price + costs) your annual mortgage interest is $54 600.

In the example that follows I've used the average interest rate, while noting that by shopping around for a better deal you could find a lower interest rate. The sharpest variable mortgage interest rates at the time of writing are sitting at 4.04 per cent, significantly lower than the average rate.

This example points out that borrowing the full purchase price as well as your costs is possible only if you're using either equity from another property or a family guarantee loan.

The reason the entire amount has been included in this example is to show you the full costs of the entire purchase. If you purchase a property with a cash deposit, it will mean your loan is smaller and mortgage repayments will be less than the preceding figures.

Property costs are tax deductible

Tax deductibles are covered in detail in chapter 7, on tax, but the short version is that if your investment property expenses are more than the rental income you receive, you can claim the difference as a tax deduction.

Based on Australian marginal tax rates, if your taxable income is above $45 000, your marginal tax rate + Medicare levy is 34.5 per cent. This means that for every dollar your investment property costs you, you'll receive a tax refund of $0.345. If your income and tax rate are higher, you'll receive even more back at tax time.

This helps to reduce the after-tax cost of running your property, as it essentially gives back at least a third of whatever you pay at tax time.

Financial benefits of an investment property

The benefits of owning an investment property are twofold. You'll get an income return through the rent paid by your tenants and you'll receive a benefit from the growth in value of your property over time.

According to CoreLogic data, the average gross rental income on property in Australian capital cities as at October 2022 was 3.36 per cent, and as previously noted the long-term growth rate on property is 6.3 per cent.

Bringing it together

Purchase costs

Property value:	$1 000 000
Purchase costs @ 5%:	$50 000
Total funds needed:	**$1 050 000**

Ongoing income

Gross annual rental income @ 3.36%:	$33 600

Ongoing expenses

Ongoing property expenses @ 1%:	−$10 000
Mortgage interest:	−$54 600
Total costs:	−$64 600
Cashflow cost/net income:	**−$31 000**
Tax refund @ 34.5%:	+$10 695
Net holding costs after tax:	**$20 305**

Property growth

Average annual growth @ 6.3%:	$63 000

Buying your dream home can make you seriously poor

The allure of buying your dream home is real. You get that warm feeling that comes from knowing you own the roof over your head. You can paint that feature wall in any shade of tangerine that strikes your fancy. You don't have to deal with annoying property managers or landlords. And you don't have to pay 'dead money' in rent.

But here's the thing: your own home is something that never really makes you money. Sure, your property might increase in value over time, but it doesn't deliver any money to your bank account until you sell it.

Assuming you're always going to need somewhere to live, once you buy your own home you probably will want to continue to own the roof over your head, so your home might not get sold while you're alive.

When you own your own home you have to cover the mortgage, rates and ongoing costs. There are no tax deductions available for the home you live in, so it will cost you more out of pocket than it would to rent the same property. And the more you spend on it, the more of your cashflow and savings capacity you direct to paying off this lovely roof over your head, and the less you'll have left over for investing.

Balance your home vs non-home assets

When looking at how much wealth you have, two measures are important. The first is your total net asset position. This is the combined value of all your assets and investments less the value of all liabilities and debts.

The other key measure is your net assets excluding your home, and is the value of all of your assets except for your home less the value of all liabilities including your home mortgage. This measure gives you the true picture of your real wealth, because it only includes assets you're using as investments that will actually deliver you financial returns you can use to replace your salary and fund your lifestyle if you're not earning a pay cheque.

For example, if someone has a total net asset position of $5 million, you might think they're doing well. But if $4.5 million of these assets is tied up in their home, their real investment wealth is only $500k, so clearly they're still a long way from financial freedom.

On the flip side, someone with $5 million in assets whose home is worth only $500k has a total investment wealth of $4.5 million. This is a vastly different picture, and this person would most likely be financially free already.

Finding the right balance between your 'home' vs your 'non-home' wealth is a critical driver of financial freedom.

I've seen a lot of people get this wrong by spending too much on their home too early on their wealth-building journey, placing them in a position where they have a much smaller amount of money left over for investing. If you fall into this trap, your progress will be slow going and hard fought.

Your own home is an expense, not an investment

In this chapter I talk a lot about property strategies and building wealth through property. But to be clear, what I'm talking about is *investing* with property, not buying your own home. Buying your own home is a decision and money strategy that should be considered separately from your investing and wealth-building strategy. And given its financial impact, you should think of it as an expense rather than an investment.

Clearly, buying your own home is closely related to your overall money plan, but given the importance of this decision and the long-term implications for your money, it warrants careful consideration and planning.

Don't get me wrong, I think buying your own home is important, valuable and something everyone should do. But the right move at the wrong time is still the wrong move, and if you get this wrong it can seriously sabotage your ability to build wealth and replace your salary through investing.

I'll cover planning around this in detail later, but to spoil the surprise (sorry), renting the home you live in first and investing to build your wealth will almost always allow you to grow your investments faster than buying your own home earlier.

I totally get that renting can be a pain, but if replacing your salary by investing is a priority, sucking it up by renting for longer might give you a serious advantage that will help you achieve your goals faster.

Of course, if you're fortunate enough to work and live somewhere where you can buy your dream home for well below the average house price in Australia, you're one of the lucky ones. This can make it much easier to comfortably afford your home earlier on in your investing journey *without* throwing a serious spanner in your investing plans. But even if you're in this enviable position, it's still important you plan carefully around your home purchase to ensure it fits with your other money goals.

The dead money myth

So many people tell me that one of the main reasons they want to buy their own home is so they can stop paying 'dead money' in rent, or that they 'don't want to be paying off someone else's mortgage'. I get the sentiment here, but it is absolutely the wrong way to look at things.

It comes from incorrectly looking at the decision around buying a property as presenting two options: option 1 is you rent the house you live in; option 2 is you buy your own home. But this perspective is missing some crucial information that will help you choose the best path forward.

Here are the two options you're really deciding between: Do you choose to rent the house you live in and because you're only paying rent and not having to cover mortgage costs and ongoing property costs, you save more money that you can invest to grow your wealth? Or do you save up a bunch of money you'll then tie up in a property deposit, take out a mortgage you need to cover every month, and pay the ongoing costs attached to owning a property, leaving you with less money to save and invest for the next 20-odd years while you pay down your home mortgage?

When you look at the decision in this light, you can see that you're not choosing *just* to pay dead money in rent or choosing *just* to pay off someone else's mortgage. Rather, you're choosing to let someone else do the heavy lifting in paying for the lovely roof over your head, so you can free up more money to direct to investing and building your wealth.

Property risk and how to manage it

There are a few different risks you'll face when you invest in property, some more easily managed than others. They include:

- spending the wrong amount on a purchase
- choosing the wrong property

- interest rate risk
- medical risk
- lifestyle risk.

Spending the wrong amount on a purchase

How much to spend on a property is something many people decide part way through the property-buying process. It should be your very first decision.

Deciding on how much you'll allocate to your investment property purchase will help guide what suburbs or states to include in your property search, whether you're aiming for an apartment or a house, and what your borrowing strategy will look like.

Deciding on your purchase price at the front end will save you a heap of time and frustration through the property-buying process and dramatically reduce the risk of letting your emotions compromise the financial outcomes of your purchase.

Property draws an emotional response, because when you look at a property it's almost impossible not to imagine yourself living there and to think about how the property 'feels' to you. But if you let your emotions get in the way of what should be a shrewd investment decision, you will likely make mistakes.

To decide on the right amount to spend, you need to look at what the purchase will mean for what you have left over. Success here means your property investment won't force you to sacrifice anything that's important to you in terms of your spending or investing capacity. What will your purchase mean for how quickly your wealth will grow post-purchase?

Later I'll dive deep into planning a property purchase (and your other investing), but for now you should know that in my opinion you should aim to spend as much as you can afford on your purchase.

The one caveat to this is that you don't want to buy into the high-end luxury property market, where rental returns relative to property values significantly reduce (discussed further below).

The exception to this may be your first investment property at the start of your journey, when getting into the market at a lower price point allows you to get into the market sooner. In this case, buying a cheaper property allows you to start building your property equity sooner, rather than waiting for years to grow a bigger deposit so you can buy a higher value property.

There are a few reasons I suggest spending as much as you can afford when you buy property. When you spend more on a property, you will get a 'better' property. You'll be able to buy in better suburbs that are more in demand. You'll get a bigger property that has a larger market pool of potential tenants and buyers when you do choose to sell.

But importantly, because the reason you're buying property is to get leveraged exposure to a quality asset, the more you spend, the greater your property starting value will be, and therefore the more it will grow over time.

You should also be aware that every investment property you own will require some level of time input from you. This can range from not much if you have a quality property with easy tenants, to a lot if you have a property that needs a lot of ongoing work or maintenance or if you have difficult tenants or need to change tenants frequently.

Even if you have the world's best property manager in place (and I can tell you from personal experience that really good ones are few and far between), you'll still need to put in some work. The more properties you own, the more work you'll have to put in.

When buying property you should aim for your ideal level of property exposure (the total value of your property) from the smallest possible number of properties. When you do this, you'll be set up for the growth you want, have higher quality investments, and have fewer projects that require your time and attention.

How to choose a good property

Once you're clear on how much you want to spend on a property, you need to choose a good one. There are a heap of different opinions and ideas around this. The volume of content you can find online is staggering. Most property gurus are adamant that their way is 'the only way' and that everyone else is wrong in their approach. But the thing is, there are a lot of different ways to be right when it comes to property.

You could chase the property hotspots, buy–renovate–flip, buy off the plan and sell for a profit before completion, build a positively geared property portfolio, target distressed properties or follow a simple buy-and-hold strategy. All these strategies can work and have worked in the past.

So I'm not going to tell you that my way is the only way, because it's not. But I'll unpack my personal strategy and the approach I advocate to the people I help with their money, and why it works for me.

The short version is this:

- Buy a premium property.
- Target as much land as possible when you buy.
- Target low ongoing property costs.
- Hold for the long term.

Follow this approach and you'll end up with a few good properties that you can hold long term, with strong rental and low vacancy rates. You'll have fewer properties so fewer headaches. You'll all but eliminate the risks of buying a dud property.

And because you're buying and holding for the long term, the work will be way less onerous than if you were buying and selling regularly. You also don't need to agonise over the right time to buy and sell, because the right time is dictated by your strategy as opposed to what's going on in the property market.

This approach is much more straightforward than most other property-buying strategies. And simple is effective.

Here I'll unpack the why behind the what.

Premium properties

I'll illustrate this one with an example from the Sydney property market because it's the market I know best.

In Sydney, the upper end of our target price range for an investment property is around $1.4 million. For this price you can get a two-bedroom apartment in Bondi Beach, Surry Hills or Mosman, maybe even with a car space.

Putting aside for a minute the silliness of Sydney's prices relative to other property markets around the country, let's look at the dynamics of this investment.

Overall, the supply of these properties is limited and the demand is strong — the two fundamental drivers of value of your investment over time.

All suburbs within five kilometres of the Sydney CBD are fully built out, and in most of these suburbs council zoning restricts large new developments. At the same time, there is strong population growth in these areas now and more projected into the future, meaning there will be more people who want to live in these areas. This drives low rental vacancy rates and protects the income from your investment property.

With this sort of property, you've also got a good market for tenants and for prospective buyers of your property. Rent won't be cheap, so your tenants are likely to be professionals working in or around the CBD in jobs that pay well, meaning you can count on a stable rental income and are less likely to have a tenant who loses their job and can't afford to pay their rent.

The resale market on the property will also be strong, with people looking to buy their first or second home, downsizers and investors, so the property should sell quickly if you want to exit, and the value will hold up well while you own it.

When you're looking at suburbs, I'd suggest sticking with those with lower density levels with fewer apartments and more houses. What this will mean is that over time as density increases, you'll benefit from the value of your property holding its current density level.

Suburbs like Green Square and Ultimo have much higher density levels, impacting property values and making them slightly less desirable from an investing perspective.

Target as much land as possible

When you buy a property, the physical bricks and mortar are not where the main value lies. It's not in the paint on the walls, your state-of-the-art oven, or the fixtures and fittings. The biggest part of the value is in the land. So the more land you own, the more the value of your property will increase over time.

When you buy a house over an apartment, you get more land. This isn't to say that apartments are never a good investment, as they have performed well over time. Also, looking at the Sydney and Melbourne property markets, planning on buying a house in your target spending range may be unrealistic.

When you buy an apartment, you own a slice of the land the apartments are built on. If you own an apartment in a block of six, you'll own one sixth of the land. If you own a unit in a block of 60 apartments, you'll own one sixtieth. If you buy in a block of 600, you'll own one six hundredth of the land. The bigger the block, the less land you own, and the less land you own the less growth you'll get over time.

Aim for lower ongoing costs

This is a simple one, but it's worth mentioning. When you buy a property, whether it's a house or an apartment, keeping your costs low makes it easier for you to 'carry' the investment. If your aim is to buy more than one investment property (as I suggest it should be), each property will draw on your cashflow. The more you spend on ongoing property expenses, the more you'll have to put in out of your own pocket.

Property features like pools, gyms and elevators are nice to have but expensive to operate and maintain. From a pure investment perspective, avoid these costly features and you'll minimise your costs and have more money left over for your next property and other investments.

Hold for the long term

Property is expensive to buy and sell, and these costs will eat into your property profits. If you buy quality properties from the start with a good strategy behind you, it's likely you'll be selling one good property only to buy another one, incurring sale and purchase costs as well as, potentially, capital gains tax. When you run the numbers this is unlikely to make much sense.

The exception is when you transition from a focus on asset and investment building to a focus on generating income from your investing. I'll discuss this in detail later. In the wealth-building phase of your journey to replace your salary by investing, I strongly recommend you buy properties you're ready to hold for the long term.

Cashflow risk

There are two main areas of risk in relation to the cashflow of an investment property: your ability to earn an income, and your ability to fund your mortgage costs.

Medical risk

Illness, injury or accident can interrupt your ability to work and generate an income. You can protect yourself with insurance such as income replacement and life insurance.

When most people think about this sort of risk and insurance, they immediately imagine having an accident or losing their job. Both of these are risks, but they're short-term risks with limited financial impact. What I'm more talking about here is long-term illness or even, in the worst case, death, both of which can cause serious financial problems for you and/or your family (along with the obvious personal impact).

A few years back my uncle, who was previously fit and healthy, was at home when he suffered a seizure. He had been healthy all his life with no serious medical issues, and this crisis came out of the blue. After he underwent a barrage of medical tests they found a brain tumour, which subsequently grew and around two years later he passed away, leaving behind a wife and three kids.

This was devastating for our family on a personal level, but thankfully my uncle had taken advice early on and had good insurance cover in place that helped to ease the financial impact.

This is an extreme example, but it does happen. Over the years, a number of my clients have been diagnosed with serious medical conditions, and some have died unexpectedly. Good insurance will protect you against the unexpected and ensure that accident or illness doesn't cause serious financial problems.

If you're buying investment properties, and particularly if you're buying multiple properties and running a reasonably high level of debt, protecting yourself and your family with, at a minimum, quality income replacement insurance and life insurance are non-negotiable in my opinion.

Insurance is a complex area and largely beyond the scope of this book, but I strongly recommend you seek out a professional financial adviser and get some good advice around your insurance cover, particularly if you're going to invest in property seriously. The complexity of insurance means it's next to impossible for most people to do this well on their own.

Interest rates

The second part of cashflow risk is around interest rates. When you buy property, you need to protect yourself against rising interest rates to make sure the purchase will continue to work for you.

At the time of writing, in November 2022, we've just seen the fastest rise in mortgage interest rates in almost 30 years, with rates increasing by 3 per cent in just seven months. This has led to many Australian mortgage holders struggling to keep up with their payments and do the other things they want with their money.

I feel for these people. I think many people are now realising they've borrowed more than they probably should have. When interest rates are low, it's easy to fall into the trap of thinking they will stay that way for a long time. But they often don't.

No one has a crystal ball, so we don't know exactly where rates will go from here, but I suggest adding 3 per cent to your current interest rate to see what your repayments would look like at that level.

It's possible this will be forced on you at some point, and if this happens you'll need to find a way to make it work. It's likely you'll need to compromise on either your spending or your saving, or both.

If you look at the numbers and they're not stacking up, you need to think again about your property purchase and whether your strategy is the right one for you. If rising interest rates would cause you problems, you could also consider fixing all or part of your mortgage to give you certainty about rates over time.

How to structure your mortgage

When you take out a mortgage, there are a couple of decisions you'll need to make around how to structure your debt. The first is whether you should use a principal and interest loan or an interest only loan. The second is whether to use a fixed interest rate or a variable rate.

Principal and interest vs interest only

With an interest only mortgage, as the name suggests, you pay only the interest on the loan with your mortgage repayments. If you run an interest only loan forever, you will never actually pay down the amount you owe (the principal).

You might ask why anyone would do this, but an interest only mortgage does have the big advantage that your mortgage repayments are significantly lower, because you're not having to put in extra money to actually reduce your debt.

You can still get ahead with an interest only loan; it's just that you're relying on the value of your property increasing over time.

For investment properties interest costs are tax deductible. If you never reduce your debt, this will mean your interest costs, and therefore your deductions, will remain higher throughout your loan. With a principal and interest (P&I) loan, your monthly mortgage repayment will cover the interest costs and repay a small amount of the principal. You pay more each month, but your debt reduces over time.

Historically, the interest rates were the same for P&I loans and interest only loans. But a few years back the Australian financial markets regulator,

APRA, recognised that if everyone was using interest only loans there would be more risk in the financial system because some people would be running higher levels of debt. In order to reduce the number of interest only loans, they put measures in place that resulted in the banks increasing the interest rates for interest only loans relative to principal and interest loans.

In my view, running an interest only mortgage is totally fine (and probably a good thing), though paying a higher interest rate makes an interest only mortgage a less attractive option. In this case, your decision is between paying an extra interest expense (and seeing that money gone forever) or saving money by paying down the principal on your loan. You want and need to be saving money over time, so paying down your principal isn't a bad thing. This way you save on interest costs—money you'll never get back.

On the other hand, an interest only loan could help you in the shorter term to afford a property you otherwise couldn't. In this case, the amount of money you make from your property investment will more than cover the extra interest costs, so you'll be way better off by going interest only.

In all other cases, personally I'd choose a P&I loan and save on interest costs.

Fixed vs variable interest rates

With a variable mortgage, the interest rate you pay will fluctuate over time based on the interest rates set by the Reserve Bank of Australia (RBA) and the banks themselves.

With a fixed interest rate, you essentially 'lock in' your interest rate for a set period of time (generally between one and five years). Fixed interest rates give you certainty on what your repayments will be, which can be valuable when you buy a property. It can give you peace of mind and go a long way to reducing stress around your ability to comfortably fund your mortgage payments *and* do the other things you want with your money.

I speak to a lot of people who think the decision between a fixed and variable rate is about 'beating the bank', but I can tell you that's a tough undertaking. In Australia, the banks have huge teams of analysts, economists and market experts who are constantly focused on how the bank should price their fixed rate mortgages to ensure they remain profitable for the business.

It's worth noting that the banks generally price their fixed rate mortgages so they make the same amount of money whether a customer uses a fixed or variable interest rate mortgage. They don't always get this right, but history shows us that the banks get it right more often than they get it wrong. So it's really hard to beat them at this game. But fixing your mortgage isn't just about beating the bank. There are other significant advantages when you fix your mortgage.

Rate rises have been priced in

At the time of writing, interest rates are on the rise coming off the back of never-before-seen lows through the COVID pandemic. Because interest rates are rising and the banks are expecting rates to rise further, fixed mortgage rates are significantly higher than variable rates. This means if you're thinking about fixing your mortgage, you need to be prepared to pay a higher rate in the short term.

So how do you work out whether fixing your mortgage is the right move for you?

Step 1: Understand the costs of fixing your mortgage

The first step in going down this path is to look at what it would cost if you were to fix your mortgage tomorrow. You can use an online comparison site, or speak with your mortgage broker or bank to confirm what your new monthly mortgage repayments would be.

Step 2: Assess how this fits with your savings and investment plan (budget)

Now you've put together a solid saving and spending plan, you'll be able to look at your budget and savings surplus to see what difference rising interest rates would make.

To consider the impact of rising interest rates on a variable mortgage, use an online mortgage calculator to see how your repayments would change if interest rates were to increase by 2 per cent or 3 per cent.

Then look at what it would cost if you were to fix your mortgage today.

Based on the outcomes you identify by going through this process, if it seems like fixing your mortgage would create financial pressure you should tread carefully. But if you look at your rising variable rate scenario and this puts you under financial stress, looking to fix some or all your mortgage might be a more comfortable path forward.

The mortgage market moves quickly, and the interest rates you can access today may not be offered tomorrow. Interest rates are currently on the way up, so if you make the decision to fix your rates you should take action promptly to lock in what's on the table.

Fixed and variable mortgage interest rates both have their advantages and disadvantages, and each has its place. Beating the banks is close to impossible, and the choices you make here will likely impact your situation for years, so it's worth taking the time to get this right.

To make the best choice for you, understand the impact of the different options and variations both today and into the future, and be sure you make a considered decision as part of your overall money plan.

Three property mistakes to avoid

Property is an area in which mistakes can be extremely costly, creating problems that can hold you back for years or even decades. Here I want to unpack the top three property mistakes I witness, so you can avoid them.

Buying off the plan

This one is a little controversial, and for good reason. Many people have made a lot of money from buying property this way, but there's one big downside I personally just can't get past.

Buying property off the plan means purchasing a property before it's built, typically through a developer. You agree on the price you'll pay for the property and sign your purchase contract before the property is finished. Then once the property is fully complete the purchase is finalised, you pay the rest of the money and the property is yours.

The advantage of buying off the plan, particularly in a rising property market, is that you 'lock in' the price of the property today, and by the time it's built it could have a higher value.

But if the property market goes down, if your property was overpriced to begin with or if mortgage rules change, you can run into serious trouble. There's also the risk of the property developer going bust in the middle of the build. These risks can have serious long-term impacts on your ability to replace your salary by investing.

In 2018 I was working with a client who had purchased a property off the plan. She bought a good house in the Hunter Valley region of NSW that was priced well and had a completion date in mid-2019. Her income was stable and increasing over time. Things were looking good, but this property purchase turned into one of the most stressful experiences I've been involved with.

The Banking Royal Commission was going on at the time and the banks were in a lot of trouble for not being robust in their assessment of people's borrowing capacities. As a result, APRA mandated how banks assessed how much their customers could borrow.

Unfortunately for my client, this reassessment meant that even though her income was increasing, her borrowing power reduced significantly. When it came time to complete the purchase, she could borrow less money and needed to scramble to make it work. In the end she had to take out a personal loan and borrow from family so she wouldn't lose the $100k+ deposit she'd put down.

This is an extreme example, but it shows how over time external circumstances can change in a way that impacts whether a property purchase remains a good idea (or even possible). When you buy off the plan this uncertainty can be seriously stressful and potentially expensive.

In today's softening property market, large numbers of people face similar difficult situations with off-the-plan properties. For anyone who contracted to purchase a property to be delivered in 2023, it's highly likely that when the property is built it will be worth less than it was when the contract was signed. This means the banks will want to lend less because the value is lower, and it's the responsibility of the buyer to cover the shortfall.

For me, this stress and pressure outweigh any potential upside from buying off the plan and they are the reason I avoid this strategy at all costs.

Investing for tax purposes alone

Buying an investment property comes with some tax perks. There's the potential for negative gearing, where you can deduct your mortgage interest and ongoing property costs. When you buy a new property, the tax deductions get even bigger through the magic of 'depreciation'.

Depreciation is the reduction in the value of the fittings and fixtures of a property over time. When you buy a new home, before you move in everything is brand new and worth the full retail replacement value.

For example, your oven might be worth $2500 when you buy it. But once you roast your first chicken, the oven is 'used', and if you were to try to sell it you might get only $2000 for it. Once you've cooked 100 roast chickens over a few years, the same oven might fetch only $1000. This reduction in value over time is called depreciation.

Depreciation doesn't really cost you money. It's not like you physically pay money out of your pocket as things in your property come to be worth less. But the tax rules allow you to claim this depreciation in value as a tax-deductible expense. This means you receive big tax deductions and part of the money back at tax time.

After the tax benefits are factored in, depreciation can transform what would be a negatively geared property that costs you money each month into a positive cashflow investment.

But I've seen people get blinded by these tax benefits and compromise on the actual property investment they're buying. If you fall into this trap, you might get some great tax deductions for a while, but over time depreciation reduces until it's gone altogether. If at the end of this period you're left with a property that's not a good investment without the tax benefits, you're going to be put in a difficult situation.

You may need to sell your property at a loss, or perhaps at a small gain, which probably doesn't sound that bad. But what you've missed out on is having a property that makes you good money in line with the long-term property market average growth rate.

I'll let you in on a little secret. If a property (or any other investment for that matter) isn't a good investment without the tax benefits, it was never a good investment to begin with. When you make any investment, the tax benefits should be the 'cream on top', not the reason you invest.

Buying new properties that have big depreciation benefits can be great, but it's critical to ensure you're buying a property that will be a good investment in itself.

Sacrificing growth for income

There's a lot of talk out there about building a positively geared property portfolio, but it can lead property buyers to make a big mistake.

Don't get me wrong, the idea of buying positive income properties is a good one. But where people go wrong is they compromise on the growth potential of a property just to get a higher rental income return.

You can see from the examples outlined in this chapter that the biggest benefit you receive from property is the growth of that property's value over time. Crucial to your success is finding properties that are going to grow at an average rate.

When you look at what sort of properties have higher rental incomes (rental yield), it's typically properties that have lower growth prospects — not always, but most of the time. For example, typically properties in regional and more remote areas will deliver a higher rental yield. At the same time, these properties typically don't grow at the same rate as a property in a capital city where the rental yield is lower.

If you can find a property that has strong growth potential and meets the criteria I've outlined here *and* has a strong rental yield, great. But it's a mistake to compromise on the growth of your property just so you can bring in an extra few bucks in rent.

Who helps you with property?

When you buy property there are some people you 'need' and others you might want. Having the right people in your corner at the right time can help you make better property decisions and mean you make more money from your property investments.

Lawyer or conveyancer

Unless you're a property law expert yourself, you'll need someone to manage the legal side of your purchase. You can use a property conveyancer or a property lawyer who will help you manage contracts and legal title transfers.

Property contracts are dense and complicated, and even some professionals can struggle with quirky clauses and conditions, so you want to have someone experienced here.

Mortgage broker or bank

If you borrow to buy property, you'll need a mortgage. You can either go to the bank directly or use a mortgage broker. Both approaches can work, but in my opinion a mortgage broker is a better option.

A mortgage broker is able to use a range of different banks and mortgage products, which will typically result in your securing a better mortgage interest rate. Mortgage brokers also help project manage the administration around setting up a mortgage, which can save you time (and frustration).

Property buyer's agent

A property buyer's agent is an expert at buying properties. They will generally help you find properties that meet your set criteria, then negotiate and secure the property for you.

The advantage of using a buyer's agent is that because they buy a lot of properties they have a strong sense of the property market and the price you should be paying, and they have more experience negotiating on properties. These factors can help you get the property you want at a lower price.

Financial adviser or financial planner

A financial adviser can help you map out your property strategy, with the aim of finding a property that will deliver the financial results and growth you want *and* fit in with your lifestyle and other money plans.

A financial planner is optional, but having a financial plan is crucial when you buy property if you want to get the best possible outcomes. At a minimum you need to be clear on how your property purchase will fit with your money today as well as into the future as your situation changes, and to be clear on the risks covered in this chapter and how you will manage and reduce them.

How to build your property professional dream team

Having the right people in your corner when you buy property gives you a serious advantage. It's critically important to have the right people to deliver the outcomes you're looking for. Refer to chapter 9 where I unpack how to find good professionals and the key screening questions to ask.

Building your property dream team sooner will help you set your strategy and get clear on your ideal property purchase timeline, most likely resulting in your getting into the property market sooner. It's never a problem having good people on standby, but if you leave it too late to set them up, you could get caught short. By building your team as soon as property comes onto your radar, you'll be better placed to get the results you want when you buy.

THE WRAP

Property is the largest single investment you'll make on your journey to replacing your salary by investing. It's also the investment that will move the dial furthest on your rate of progress.

There's a lot of information for you to be across here, but property is an area you have to get right if you want to come close to achieving your financial potential.

It's also an area where the difference between doing 'okay', 'good' and 'great' can be counted in the hundreds of thousands (potentially millions) of dollars, so it's worth taking all the time you need to nail it.

Your action plan

- [ ] Reread the start of this chapter so you're clear on the power of leverage and how it can help you build your assets.

- [ ] Create your property-investing mandate: what type of properties you'll buy and where.

- [ ] Understand your borrowing capacity today and how this is likely to change over time by speaking with a mortgage broker or financial adviser.

- [ ] Lay out how much it will cost you to run an investment property and how it fits in with your plan to replace your salary.

- [ ] Map out your property market entry point and a timeline to get there.

- [ ] Create a property risk management plan to protect yourself and your property purchase.

- [ ] Build your property professional dream team and seek guidance early.

- [ ] Start investing!

—

CHAPTER 5

Crypto, bro?

Cryptocurrency and digital assets have exploded onto the investing landscape around the globe in recent years, and no surprises why.

In the past 10 years, the total value of all cryptocurrency (crypto) increased over 193 000 per cent from less than US$1.5 billion to over US$2.9 *trillion* by the end of 2021. Since then it has experienced a period of steep decline, falling to a value of just US$950 million.

Since inception the ups and downs of crypto have been huge, but over the long term the upward trajectory is clear. In recent years in particular we've seen its adoption as a form of payment by a bunch of big groups, including Tesla, PayPal and even the entire country of El Salvador. The 'validation' of crypto by these big players is shifting public opinion, and we're now seeing people of all ages investing in greater numbers than ever before.

Along with this increase in value and the future potential gains, there has been a lot of press attention, leading many Aussies to question whether crypto should be part of their investment portfolio.

But cryptocurrency and digital investments are complex, and the Web 3.0 space is rapidly evolving, which makes it hard for would-be crypto investors to understand what you really need to know to figure out if crypto makes sense for you.

First, I'm going to make something really clear: you don't need to invest in crypto or digital assets. If you never invest a single dollar in the digital assets market, but follow the other principles and strategies in this book, you will reach your goal of successfully replacing your salary by investing.

Crypto should absolutely be *considered* by anyone looking to invest, but sometimes things should be considered just so you can confidently rule them out.

If you choose not to invest in crypto, it will be because you have examined the option and decided against adopting it. If you do choose to invest some money in crypto, you'll have a clear strategy. Either way, you'll be confident in your choice and can then focus closely on your chosen investment strategy and avoid the noise from other investors, the media or people in your circle.

In my opinion, the crypto and digital asset space is an interesting one with a future, and there may be an opportunity to invest with crypto in a smart, informed way.

A word on terminology. *Digital assets* is the broad term used for all cryptocurrencies. *Non-fungible tokens (NFTs)*, *tokens* and *stablecoins* also point to assets in the crypto world. In this chapter I use these terms more or less interchangeably, while drawing attention to any important distinctions.

Table 5.1 compares the returns on the two largest cryptocurrencies with Australian and US shares as at October 2022.

Table 5.1 Returns on shares vs cryptocurrency

	1yr (%)	3yr (%)	5yr (%)
Australian shares	−11.09	+0.42	+15.09
S&P 500 (US)	−17.91	+23.58	+44.71
Nasdaq (US)	−29.07	+30.94	+61.05
Bitcoin	−69.22	+106.66	+232.95
Ethereum	−61.05	+699.41	+428.91

You can see from this table that the long-term return on cryptocurrency is higher than that on shares, but that the downside risk is also much higher.

How much risk do you need?

When you invest you aim to make as much money as possible from your investment. But what many people don't think about as much as they should is how much risk you *need* to take to get the results you want.

Going back to the example used in chapter 3, starting with $0 in your investment account at age 20, if you were to save and invest $10.10 daily, then reinvest all income (dividends on your shares) over time, by the time you reach age 60 you'd have built total investments of $1 840 592 — enough to replace the average salary with investment income.

This figure is based on the long-term return of the regular share market only, and shows that you don't need your investments to make you more of a return to create serious wealth.

So the question then becomes, how much risk do you need?

If you want to grow from where you are today to your ideal future wealth level to replace your ideal salary through investing, you have two options. You can choose a path that might get you there faster. This path may be fast, but you have a higher chance of suffering serious setbacks that could kill your money momentum and send you back to the starting line. Or you can choose a path that might take slightly longer but will give you a much higher chance of getting there.

For me, the second path is the smarter play. But our money psychology and inner investor pushes us to want more and want it faster, which can lead us to make investment choices that carry more risk, driving stress and frustration, and ultimately losing money.

If you have some clear investing targets you're working towards, instead of pushing to get there as quickly as possible and running a heap of risk in the process, think through how you could get there with the highest degree of *certainty* possible. You'll likely find your investment approach will change as a result.

That said, personally I find the crypto and digital asset space fascinating, and I believe the value of digital assets like cryptocurrency will continue to grow into the future. I also believe that if you're smart about how you tackle digital asset investing, you can fit crypto into a bigger picture plan in a way that potentially offers an upside without taking on a level of risk you don't need.

Where people go wrong with cryptocurrency and digital assets

When you get serious about investing and money, your aim is to build wealth in a way that sustainably provides for the lifestyle you want to live. Like building a house, you need to start with the foundations and get your basic building blocks in place before you start building the upper levels.

You need a solid spending and saving plan to set the platform for your investing, and a game plan for getting some solid investments behind you to start delivering compound growth year on year. And you need to be smart with your planning and optimise your situation and investment progress.

In the early days of building your investments, you want to stock your investment portfolio with rock-solid investments. You should be able to sleep like a baby at night, knowing your investments will do their thing and grow for you. Sure, any share and property investments will follow the ups and downs of the market, but you should never need to question whether they will come back. Your investments should also be delivering a regular income stream you can reinvest to grow your wealth.

One of the main areas where I've seen people go wrong with crypto is going all in on digital assets too early in their investing journey. It's easy to get drawn in by the allure of making a bunch of money quickly, so you allocate more money into high-risk crypto investments.

Go down this path and you could make a heap of money quickly, but could also lose a lot just as fast. Witnessing downturns like the one from late 2021 through 2022, you can see that crypto can create as many losers as winners.

Once you have a solid foundation of investments in place, a share portfolio in the six-figure range, and property investments in place, crypto can be a move that fits in with your wealth building in a way that doesn't compromise your chances of success.

What is cryptocurrency?

The basis of the majority of cryptocurrencies like Bitcoin and other digital assets is blockchain, which is a technology that has been around since 1991. Bitcoin was introduced in 2009 and has since grown phenomenally in popularity.

Types of digital assets

There are many different types of digital assets, and the surrounding terminology and jargon can be overwhelming. I want to give you a basic understanding of your digital asset investment options by unpacking the most common digital assets and how they can be used.

Web 3.0 investment funds

These funds use traditional investments such as ETFs and managed funds to invest either directly in digital assets or in companies that play in the Web 3.0 space. They're newer to the scene, but more and more of them are being launched. They give investors easy access to the digital asset markets without the need for understanding blockchain technology and how to physically trade in digital assets. They offer an easy entry point to digital asset investing.

Cryptocurrency

The original digital asset, these are any digital store of value or currency that's stored on the blockchain. Cryptocurrency can be used for payments, investing or creating a coin to fund a project.

Non-fungible tokens (NFTs)

This is a token that is essentially like an ownership certificate for a unique digital item (say, a work of art). NFTs can be used for verifying ownership of virtual items, proving your identity or even tracking inventory.

Central bank digital coins (CBDCs)

These are cryptocurrencies like Bitcoin that are issued by a central bank (such as the Reserve Bank of Australia), although not all countries issue these digital currencies. CBDCs can be used for payments and transfers within a country or internationally.

Security tokens

These are digital assets that meet the definition of a security, like shares or stocks and bonds. Security tokens can be used as digital versions of real-world assets like property and equipment, or digital versions of more traditional assets such as shares and bonds.

Stablecoins

These are cryptocurrencies that are linked to the price of things like traditional currencies, commodities or other crypto assets. They are designed for price stability, although this stability is not guaranteed and comes with risks (similar to staking risk, which I'll discuss shortly). Stablecoins can be used as a form of payment, as well as for foreign exchange and international transfers.

Choosing between types of digital assets

While I've unpacked some detail around the various types of digital assets you can invest in here, you should know that I'm not suggesting that all or any of them necessarily have a place on your journey to replace your salary by investing.

In my opinion, the complexities and risks with all but the most basic of digital assets mean they're not a smart move for most investors. I myself have only a small investment in direct cryptocurrency and feel that this is probably appropriate for 99 per cent of people who want to invest in digital assets.

The only other option I feel is worth considering over time once you've built a solid level of wealth is the NFT space, which I find intriguing. NFTs are definitely high on the risk spectrum, though, so shouldn't be considered lightly.

What are the risks with buying cryptocurrency?

All investments have risk attached to them; as discussed, risk is what makes you money when you invest. Investing in crypto is risky, but so is buying shares and property. Even doing nothing comes with its own risks.

But given the unregulated nature and complexity of the cryptocurrency markets, there are some key risks you should be across if you're thinking about jumping on the digital asset bandwagon.

Volatility risk and asset class risk

The first big risk to be aware of is the 'volatility' or ups and downs in the value of crypto, which is significantly higher than for more traditional investments in shares and property.

This volatility risk is driven by a number of factors. Positive or negative news (around, say, Elon Musk or the threat of regulation) can have a heavy impact on market prices. If a large crypto investor needs to sell their position, this can 'move the market' and change prices significantly, given most crypto trading platforms or 'exchanges' deal mainly with smaller scale investors. Security breaches and crypto seizures are another significant price driver.

No income risk

In contrast to the more traditional investments of shares, property and cash, digital assets generally don't pay an ongoing investment income. Cryptocurrency 'staking', which I will address separately, is one exception to this.

Investment income reduces risk by ensuring that even if the value of your investments decreases, your investments are still generating income that can be used to drive investment returns. Because digital assets don't typically pay an ongoing income, if there is a decline in investment values for a prolonged period, to avoid selling at a loss you may be forced to hold an investment that isn't really working for you for a long time. Ultimately this will slow down your progress.

Staking risk

Cryptocurrency 'staking' is a relatively new concept introduced with the creation of a new cryptocurrency called 'Peercoin' in 2012. It's quite complicated and technical, but essentially staking cryptocurrency means you 'pledge' to hold a certain cryptocurrency with a provider to help that provider validate transactions on the blockchain.

As new blocks are created on the blockchain, the participants who help to validate transactions are rewarded through the issue of new cryptocurrencies, meaning people who 'stake' their crypto are paid a return, typically in cryptocurrency, for their participation.

Staking income returns can be significant, with some providers offering returns of up to 20 per cent. But staking comes with considerable risk, the greatest arising if the value of the cryptocurrency you're holding declines significantly while it's being staked.

Through 2021, when the cryptocurrency market was rising strongly, many investors entered into staking and ultimately paid the price. The most notable collapse was with UST/Terra/LUNA in 2022, when investors lost a total of US$45 billion almost overnight. Many of these investors didn't understand the risks and complexities they were getting involved with before jumping in.

The full details and complexity of crypto staking are beyond the scope of this book, but keep in mind that crypto staking involves significant risks that should be carefully considered by prospective investors. In my opinion, staking isn't a smart move for anyone who's not an experienced Web 3.0 participant.

Counterparty risk

The next risk involves the fact that most crypto is held in a 'digital wallet', which means it's effectively being 'minded' for you by someone else. This is in contrast to a share portfolio in Australia, which is held safely by a company regulated under the Australian financial market regulator APRA, where there is next to no risk of your investments going missing owing to the high level of investor protections in place.

Another aspect of this risk relates to the fact that there are a large number of crypto exchanges based out of different countries, which means if something goes wrong it can be hard to chase down your cash.

Then, given the currency is entirely digital, there's the risk of breach by hackers or other agents. This risk is amplified by the fact that data (from trend watchers such as Cardify) shows over a third of crypto investors don't fully understand the technology. This makes this particular risk very real, and one you should manage if you're thinking about joining the crypto buyers' club.

Where cryptocurrency fits in a smart investment portfolio

Even with the above risks, there's little doubt there are investment opportunities in the crypto market, and long-term crypto investors are well rewarded for their support.

The fact there is limited supply of bigger cryptocurrencies like Bitcoin and Ethereum, coupled with the accelerating broad adoption by big players, suggests strong upside potential in the coming years. That said, if you want to be smart and to sleep soundly at night, it's important you understand where crypto fits in your investment portfolio.

A big part of answering this question goes back to understanding your risk appetite, what sort of investor you are, and who you have supporting your investment decisions.

If you don't have a high risk tolerance, if you're the sort of investor who can fall into the hard-to-avoid herd mentality, or if you don't have an investment or financial adviser to help you make smart decisions, you might want to reconsider whether crypto is for you. But if you have your bases covered, understand the risks and have some good support, there is a role crypto can play for smart investors.

How to manage risk if you buy cryptocurrency and digital assets

Risk can be managed, but it can't be eliminated altogether. Digital assets have some slightly quirky risks you should be aware of, and if you're going to invest in this space it's important you understand how to manage and reduce them.

Foundations first

I've mentioned that an important part of smart investing is to have a solid foundation in place before you start getting too exotic. Crypto is not the sort of investment you should consider until you've purchased at least one investment property *and* have a solid share portfolio behind you.

Only invest a small proportion of your total wealth

I view cryptocurrencies and digital assets as high-risk, high-potential-reward investments that are speculative in nature. Investing here could pay off big time, but it could also be a total bust, so you need to manage your downside.

One way you can do this is by setting a maximum percentage of your investments in any particular area. Once you have your solid investing foundation behind you, if you're particularly interested in crypto investing you could nominate a small, set proportion of your future investments that you'll direct to the digital asset space.

It might be anywhere from 1 per cent to 5 per cent of your future investments, depending on how keen you are and how this investing fits in with your next big money move. Any more than 5 per cent of your total ongoing investments involves more risk than you really need (or should want) in your investment portfolio.

Stick to the big players

My personal investment philosophy, and the one I recommend to the people I help as a financial adviser, is to stick to 'blue chip' investments when you're looking to build wealth. For shares, this means investing in big, quality companies with a strong track record. For property, this means choosing quality properties in good suburbs that have performed well over the long term. And when it comes to crypto and digital assets, this means sticking to the big, more established players.

As in the share market, when you invest in small companies you have the potential for a big payday, but your risk is higher. Not all small companies survive, let alone thrive, so your chances of a huge success are lower than your chances of mediocrity or total failure.

If you decide to invest in a small new player from among the huge numbers of new cryptocurrencies being launched all the time, it's possible you will land a big payday, but you might also hit a bust.

At the time of writing, the only two cryptocurrencies I'd personally invest in are Bitcoin and Ether. These are the two largest cryptocurrencies by value. They've both been around for a long time, with Bitcoin being the first widely adopted cryptocurrency and Ether not far behind. This track record and history gives them a higher probability of standing the test of time. Their relatively large size means there's slightly less risk when the market is going down, because investors are less likely to 'give up' on these cryptos and run for the exits.

Have an emergency fund

Statistics from ME Bank found more than one in five Aussie households have less than $1000 in an emergency fund, which is scary when you're looking to invest. If you invest without a cash buffer behind you, if you need to take money out of your investments when the market is in a down period, you'll be forced to crystallise a loss and could cost yourself a packet in the process.

Before you invest, put some money aside to cover unexpected costs. This way you'll protect yourself from being forced to sell at the wrong time.

Only invest money you don't need to touch

Cryptocurrency can be volatile, so if you invest money you need to access at some point in the near future it's possible the market will be down at that point, and if you're forced to sell you'll end up losing. This is important for all investments, but given the extra volatility risk in digital assets it's especially so in this space.

Take the time to lay out what money you need for your day-to-day spending, then think ahead to any bigger costs you might have coming up to get clear on how much money you have left over that can be invested for the long term. This way when you pull the trigger on investing, you'll have the peace of mind that you won't get caught short.

Minimise your 'sells'

You only lose money on an investment when you sell. If you have a good investment, and you're able to leave that investment to bubble away for some years, you can let it do what good investments do over the long term, which is make you a bunch of money.

When you're buying and selling investments regularly, you increase your risk of losing money with every 'sell' you're involved in. Minimising your selling will take you a long way towards becoming a successful long-term investor.

Understand and stay on top of your crypto tax

Cryptocurrencies and digital assets are investments like any other when it comes to tax, and managing your tax well is important to avoid nasty surprises in the future.

Investment tax essentially works under the honour system, with taxpayers legally required to report on their investments when they do their tax return. If you don't report, then the ATO might not immediately know and you could pay less tax. But if you're audited and the ATO finds that you didn't report something, they will come after you for back taxes and possibly even penalties on top.

In recent years, as technology has drastically improved, the ATO has begun to verify transactions against the data reported by taxpayers. For example, all banks now report to the ATO the interest income paid on bank accounts, and this is matched against your tax file number so the ATO can validate when you do your tax return.

Because the cryptocurrency and Web 3.0 space is relatively new, rapidly evolving and still largely unregulated, it's difficult for the ATO to track all digital asset transactions in real time.

Some crypto investors imagine that because cryptocurrency is touted as an 'anonymous' currency it can't be traced so don't report on their investment transactions, thinking they can fly under the radar and avoid paying the tax they owe. This is a bad idea.

At the core of blockchain (which all cryptocurrencies are tied to) is a centralised register of every transaction that takes place. This means there's a permanent record of every cryptocurrency buy, sell and transfer. The ATO have specifically said they're looking closely at this space, and once they figure out exactly how best to track every digital asset transaction they'll be able to look back at the years that have passed.

When this happens, some crypto investors will be in for some nasty surprises and large tax bills. For the investor, the big risk here is that you get a huge tax bill at a time you weren't expecting it, which can jeopardise your investment plans and strategies.

If you do invest in crypto, keep good records and make sure you report all your crypto transactions to the ATO when you submit your tax return. There are a heap of good technology solutions that can help you track your crypto tax easily so it doesn't have to be hard, but it is something you need to stay on top of.

Choose a good platform

The crypto investing market works a little differently from the share market, and these differences are important to understand if you want to buy and sell crypto.

When you invest in shares listed on the ASX, it doesn't really matter what share broker you use. You could use an online broker such as Pearler, SelfWealth, CommSec or Etrade, or a traditional stockbroker working for a large bank or financial institution.

All of these brokers trade in the same share market, the Australian Stock Exchange (ASX). By contrast, when you buy and sell crypto through a cryptocurrency exchange, you're transacting with people who trade in the *same* crypto exchange. You're not trading with everyone else in the crypto world, but only with the people on the specific exchange you've chosen.

Choosing a small exchange can be risky, because you might not be getting the best possible price. For example, the price of Bitcoin may be $30k, but on any given platform there may not be any other investor willing to sell for less than $31k or buy for more than $29k.

This means choosing your exchange is an important decision, because it will dictate how sharp your buy and sell pricing is. A bigger crypto exchange will generally have more participants and offer prices closest to the market price, whereas smaller exchanges can mean the price varies more from the market price.

If you're going down the crypto path, do your research and find a large exchange to get a better deal.

Take your crypto 'off exchange'

When you invest in regulated investments like shares, ETFs, managed funds and micro-investing, your actual investments are held safely by a 'custodian' under APRA's investor protections. This means if any company in which you invest goes bankrupt your investments aren't at risk.

Crypto and digital assets are different. The default setting for all crypto exchanges is that once you buy crypto or other digital assets, they're held by the exchange. This creates a significant counterparty risk, because if the exchange goes down, your digital asset investments could go down with it.

You can protect yourself against this risk by moving any digital assets 'off exchange' to an online or offline 'wallet' where they can be held more securely. The full details around this are again beyond the scope of this book, but if you're seriously looking to play in the crypto space you should learn how this works and whether it's right for you.

THE WRAP

There's no doubt the cryptocurrency and digital assets space is an interesting one, and given its massive growth it's definitely worth considering as part of your plan to replace your salary by investing.

But just because something is worth thinking about doesn't mean it's the right move for you. And once again, the right move at the wrong time is the wrong move, so tread carefully here.

If you choose not to invest in digital assets, you should do it from a place of understanding. That way the next time there's a big crypto run or it's being spoken about more widely in the media, you'll avoid getting caught up in the hype and second guessing your strategy.

If you choose to invest in digital assets, educate yourself and follow the risk management principles covered in this chapter to give yourself the best chance of success.

There are many ways to be right when it comes to investing, but there's only one way that's right for you. Choose well, and have confidence in the path you've chosen.

Your action plan

- Get clear on the risks and potential upside of crypto by rereading this chapter and learning more.

- Understand the different types of digital assets and their upside and risks.

- Think through whether digital assets are something you think should be included in your investment strategy today or in the future.

- If you're planning to invest in digital assets, set your target wealth percentage for how much you'll hold in digital assets.

- Choose the digital assets you want to invest in.

- Map out your digital asset risk management plan.

- Select a quality exchange through which to purchase your crypto and open an account.

- Set up your initial and/or regular investment plan.

- Consider taking your crypto 'off exchange' to reduce counterparty risk.

CHAPTER 6

Sort your super

If you're like most young people, you think superannuation is something pretty boring that only matters when you're old. And if you've got aspirations of retiring early, it's easy to think the right move is to all but ignore your super and instead focus on other ways to build your wealth. And you're right...

Well, at least half right.

You absolutely should have most of your focus on investing in areas *other* than your super fund. But your super fund will grow to be one of your biggest investments, so it deserves some attention, though a little bit goes a long way here.

I want to share an example to motivate you. If you're 20, making extra super contributions of just $5 daily will mean an extra $584 391 in your super fund by age 60. And it gets better, because you can get a tax deduction for contributing to your super, which means it won't actually cost you five dollars to get five dollars into your super fund.

Over the years I've been helping people with their investing, particularly those in their 20s, 30s and 40s, I've identified a mystery that's always fascinated me.

Any sane person who has $10 000, $50 000 or $100 000 (or more) in an investment account would pay serious attention to this money. You'd want to check in on your money regularly, to know how it was invested and how your investments were performing, and you'd want to know it was set up in the best way possible.

But when it comes to super, most people take the opposite approach. Recent statistics from Finder.com.au show 10 per cent of super fund members *never* check their super fund balance, while another third of super fund members check their balance less than once every three months. To add to this, 58 per cent of Australians don't actively choose their super fund, instead going with whatever default super option is offered by their employer.

In my opinion this is borderline crazy.

I want to make something really clear here: *superannuation is YOUR money.*

Essentially, you have total control over how your super money is invested, where this money goes and how it grows. And it doesn't matter to anyone else (read your employer or super fund provider) how your super money performs and grows as much as it should matter to you.

Your super fund shouldn't need a lot of your attention or time. But at the very least take the time to choose a good super fund, set it up with quality investments and check in on how it's performing over time.

There are also a few key rules you should be aware of and tactics you can use to accelerate your journey to replacing your salary by investing.

Super is a tax structure

The government wants you to be independently wealthy. This isn't necessarily out of benevolence, but because when people are wealthy they rely on welfare less (or not at all) and they pay more taxes. The net impact is a strongly positive one on government revenue and the economy.

To increase the incentives and likelihood of people becoming wealthy, the government provides tax concessions for different types of investors. Superannuation is an area that offers among the most beneficial tax concessions, because the government knows when you save strongly through superannuation it greatly increases your chances of long-term financial security and independence—and therefore you're being a positive contributor to their profit and loss statement in the future.

Superannuation is nothing more than an investing structure with concessional tax treatment and rules on when and how you can access your money.

I'll dive deep into tax and tax strategy in the next chapter, but for now to illustrate the benefits you can access through super, table 6.1 shows the different tax rates for investing through super as opposed to investing in your personal name.

Table 6.1 Personal vs superannuation tax rates

	Income (i.e. interest and dividends)	Capital gains <12 months	Capital gains >12 months
Personal	Marginal tax rates of up to 47%	Marginal tax rates of up to 47%	Marginal tax rates of up to 47% with 50% discount
Superannuation	15%	15%	10%

As you can see from this table, investing through your superannuation means you pay a much lower rate of tax on your investment income, which ultimately helps you grow your investments faster.

And it gets even better. Once you hit age 60 and start a super pension, there is no tax payable on the earnings of the first $1.7 million in investments you have in super. AND, when you take an income from this super pension the income isn't taxed *at all*. Your super, in effect, becomes like a tax-free investment account.

Consider this example. You grow your investments to the point where they generate income of $10 000 per month. If these investments were owned in your personal name, under the FY22–23 marginal tax rates you'd pay tax on this annual income of $31 897.

If instead you were to earn this money in your super fund, the income would be received entirely tax free, saving you tax of over $2658 every single *month*. The tax benefits of super are significant.

This shows that *where* you own your investments and *where* you earn your income makes a big difference to your after-tax return. It also highlights the fact you can be 'wealthier' with the same amount of money, if you're smart about how it's structured.

Let me illustrate this further with an example comparing how an investment portfolio would grow outside of super vs inside the super environment.

To make this comparison we need to look at the *after-tax* return on each option. For this I'll use the 30-year return on the Australian share market of 9.8 per cent, which is the return before any tax is applied.

Investing in your personal name, under the current tax rules, if you're earning the Australian average income of $92 029 you'd be firmly in the $45k to $120k tax bracket, meaning you'd pay a marginal tax rate (+ Medicare levy) of 34.5 per cent. This would bring your after-tax investment return (total return less tax) to 6.42 per cent (9.8%*[1–34.5%]). On the other hand, investing through superannuation would mean your after-tax return would be 8.33 per cent (9.8%*[1–15%]).

Comparing the two using a compound interest calculator, I'm going to look at two scenarios. Both are based on a 30-year-old with $50000 they're looking to invest, with regular ongoing investments of $805 per month. In the first scenario the individual is investing in their personal name (not through superannuation), and in the second the investing is happening within superannuation.

For context, the reason the $50k starting balance has been chosen is that it is roughly the average super fund balance for a 30-year-old. The regular investment of $805 per month is based on the current compulsory employer super contribution rate of 10.5 per cent for someone earning the average Australian income of $92029.

Table 6.2 shows the numbers.

Table 6.2 After-tax growth on super vs non-super investments

Years	5	10	15	20	25	30
Personal	$125642	$229825	$373319	$570958	$843171	$1218097
Superannuation	$135384	$264694	$460530	$757116	$1206284	$1886533
Super upside	$9742	$34869	$87211	$186158	$363113	$668436

These figures show that building your investments through superannuation will mean you go further and faster than investing in your personal name. This alone means super should command more of your attention than it does right now.

Super won't be your first investing strategy

We can see from these figures that the tax benefits of superannuation are compelling. However, it's probably not the best strategy to go 'all-in' on at the start of your journey to replace your salary by investing, because you can't access your super money until age 60 under the current rules.

This means, in my view, that before you start heavily cranking your superannuation you should lay the groundwork for your investing and wealth building outside of superannuation. Specifically, your first focus early on your investment building journey should be on setting up a clear path to getting onto the property ladder. This will make a bigger difference to your long-term wealth position than the tax benefits offered by superannuation.

That doesn't mean you should do nothing about your super. Making sure your super money is invested well is something every single person should do immediately. It's also generally a good idea to start some level of extra contributions to your super fund, even if they're small and you don't think they'll make a difference—because they will.

By making extra contributions to super, you start developing good investing habits that you can then build on for the future. And as a bonus (not that you needed it) I guarantee that when you start making any level of extra contributions to your super you'll start paying more attention to your super money, which in turn will have a positive impact on how your super grows over time.

You have full control over your super investments

A common and costly super myth is that superannuation is a type of investment in and of itself. It's not. Super is its own unique investment *account* that has special tax rules, but ultimately it's just an investment account.

There are over 140 super fund providers in Australia, with more new entrants coming into the market every year. And across these funds, there are thousands of investment options you can choose from, including 'pre-mixed' options like the default investments offered by most funds, as well as specific options for Australian shares, international shares, big companies, small companies, ETFs, bonds and everything in between.

You can access virtually any investment you could invest in your personal name through your superannuation, so it all comes down to the fund you choose. Later in the chapter I'll cover exactly how to choose the best super fund and investments for you, but for now you should know that you essentially have the same amount of control over your super investments that you do over any other investment you might put your money into.

The power is in your hands, so instead of feeling like you don't have control or influence over your super, know that you absolutely do.

A note on default super options

According to data reported by the *Australian Financial Review*, 60 per cent of the 23.2 million Australian super accounts are invested in the default super fund option. I get that this is an easy option, but in my opinion it's probably not the best one for most people. In fact, more than 99 per cent of the clients we've helped build a considered financial plan that includes their superannuation have chosen an option that wasn't the default option provided by their current super fund.

The main issue with default super options is that they're stocked full of investments into things like private equity, infrastructure and other, more exotic investments that most people don't necessarily want or need. These investments are expensive and don't have a consistent track record of strong performance. And when there's a share market or economic downturn, the value of these investments is more heavily impacted than 'regular' investments like shares and property.

That said, your default option may very well be the best one for you, but you shouldn't just assume this is the case. Instead, make an active choice to get the most out of one of your largest investments.

Super contributions are tax deductible

In Australia there are two main ways you can contribute to super. One is called a 'concessional contribution', which is a contribution where someone claims a tax deduction. This type of contribution includes money contributed by your employer under the compulsory super guarantee rules, and in this case they claim a tax deduction for these contributions.

But you can make your own 'concessional contributions', either through 'salary sacrifice' contributions which are organised by your employer, or through contributions directly from your bank account, which you can then claim as a tax deduction.

The annual limit for concessional contributions today is $27 500.

As mentioned, earning the Australian average income of $92 029 means annual compulsory employer contributions of $9663. Based on the current concessional contribution limit you can make further tax-deductible contributions of $17 837 every single year.

Contributing this amount reduces your taxable income in the ATO's eyes, giving you a tax deduction for this amount. For someone earning this level of income your marginal tax rate + Medicare levy is 34.5 per cent, meaning you'd receive a reduction in your personal tax bill of $6154 each and every year.

It's worth noting that concessional contributions to super are subject to 'contribution tax' at a rate of 15 per cent, which unfortunately can't be avoided. Yes, this seems unfair, but these are the rules, and a tax rate of 15 per cent is still much lower than standard marginal tax rates.

Applying this contribution tax to the previous example, making a contribution of $17 837 would result in super contributions tax of $2676.

But overall you're still way ahead. The total tax benefit to you is the personal tax saving less the tax paid by your super fund.

Breaking it down:

• Personal tax saving:	$6154
• Tax in superannuation:	$2676
• Annual net tax benefit to you:	$3478

This saving is money you can use to grow your investments and wealth faster. Even better, once the money is invested inside the superannuation environment, it will grow at a faster rate because of the lower rate of tax on investment income inside super.

I fully appreciate that finding an extra $17 837 to contribute to your super every year would be a challenge for most people, but I wanted to show you the power of what was possible if you push it as far as you can. Contributing less will still have a powerful impact on how quickly your superannuation grows.

Consider this example.

In our previous example of a 30-year-old earning the average income with a $50k super starting balance, I looked at the impact over time of making an extra super contribution of just $5 every day. Table 6.3 sets out the results.

Table 6.3 Upside of extra super contributions

Years	5	10	15	20	25	30
Super @ 8.33%	$135 384	$264 694	$460 530	$757 116	$1 206 284	$1 886 533
Contributing + $5 per day	$146 500	$292 647	$513 980	$849 181	$1 356 831	$2 125 648
Difference	$11 116	$27 953	$53 450	$92 065	$150 547	$239 115

Once again, we see how small moves can make a big difference over time.

'Catch-up' concessional contributions

For people with a super fund balance below $500000, you can also 'catch up' on your unused contributions from previous years, contributing up to five years' worth of your unused contribution cap amount in one year.

This creates an opportunity for some serious super building and tax saving at the same time. I unpack how to use this strategy in detail in the next chapter.

After-tax contributions

Another way to build your super that isn't as well known as it could be is through making after-tax or 'non-concessional' contributions. These contributions have a separate limit, in addition to the concessional contribution limit, which under the current rules is $110000 per annum, meaning you can get some serious money into your super—if you have it lying around ready to invest.

While these contributions don't give you a tax deduction, they do get money into superannuation where the future earnings are taxed at the reduced rates previously outlined.

Given the concessional contributions allow for a significant amount of money to be contributed to your super, this probably isn't a go-to strategy for most people. Nevertheless, as you're progressing on your journey to replace your salary by investing there may be points where you have substantial money you want to invest (say, having sold a property or received an inheritance), and you may want to consider investing it through the low-tax super environment.

First home buyer super hacks

For first home buyers, there are even more benefits to contributing to super on top of these super tax strategies. The first home super saver scheme (FHSS) allows you to save for the deposit on your first property through super, and since you can contribute to super with pre-tax money you can accelerate how quickly you build your deposit.

The first home super saver scheme can help you save part or all of your property deposit with pre-tax income, helping you get into the property market sooner.

How this scheme works is that you can make extra tax-deductible contributions of up to $50k per person to your super fund, then withdraw this money and the investment earnings generated in super, and use this to purchase your first home. For couples, the benefit can be combined to leverage up to $100k in super savings, giving you a solid deposit for your first home.

The contributions you can use for this are limited to $15k in any given year and a total of $50k. Because the timeline is based on financial years, if you're smart about how you plan you can take advantage of these rules quickly.

For example:

- June 2023 (FY23) — you contribute $15k to your super fund
- July 2023 (FY24) — you contribute another $15k
- July 2024 (FY25) — you contribute another $15k
- Total contributions of $45k, all made within 14 months.

This strategy can work well if you're looking to buy your first home and *already* have your deposit saved. In this case, you could choose to not use the FHSS and to pay your deposit in the regular way. Or instead, with a bit of planning and prep, you could use the scheme and save yourself $7500 in tax in the process.

It's worth noting you can choose to save your home deposit through super more slowly if it works with your strategy. For example, you could contribute $5k each year through your 20s, then by the time you reach age 30 you'd have a total of $50k (plus your investment earnings) you could withdraw to buy your first home.

When you make the contributions to your super under this scheme, if they're done pre-tax (that is, you claim a tax deduction), they're taxed in your super fund at a rate of 15 per cent. When you withdraw funds from your superannuation, the money is taxed at your marginal tax rate less a 30 per cent tax offset.

It gets a little complicated here but you're essentially saving up to an additional 15 per cent of any amount you contribute. Based on the FHSS cap of $50k, this 15 per cent tax saving equates to $7500 (per person)—a decent chunk of change that can be a big help for someone just about to enter the property market.

There are two main risks with this strategy. Firstly, because the assumed rate of return is positive regardless of what actually happens to your investments, if your fund investments go down you can withdraw more than the money you put in. This can deplete your super savings and put you behind the curve.

The second big risk is felt by younger people in particular if their income and marginal tax rate increase over time.

The FHSS tax works as follows:

- When you contribute, you receive a tax deduction at your marginal tax rate and your super fund pays tax at the super contribution tax rate of 15 per cent, meaning the total benefit is your *current* marginal tax less 15 per cent.
- When you withdraw from the fund, the withdrawal is taxed at your *current* marginal tax rate with a 30 per cent tax offset.

If your marginal tax rate at the time of your contributions and withdrawals is the same, the total benefit to you will be 15 per cent. But if your marginal tax rate is higher when you withdraw the funds, the benefit is reduced. In fact, it can be lost altogether and you can end up behind.

Consider this example:

- Your marginal tax rate when contributing to the scheme is 19 per cent, meaning the benefit to you of contributing is (marginal tax rate – 15 per cent) 4 per cent.
- Your marginal tax rate when withdrawing under FHSS is 47 per cent, meaning the tax applied on the withdrawal is (marginal tax rate – 30 per cent) 17 per cent.

- The result is that you end up paying an *additional* 13 per cent tax on this money; based on total contributions of $50k this would be $6500 in extra tax.

You can see that it's possible to wipe out the tax benefit and end up with a tax bill to boot. This can work to your advantage if your tax rate is on the way down, but for younger people it's more commonly the other way around so you need to plan carefully.

On the flip side of this risk, there's also an opportunity if your tax rate is lower in the year you withdraw under the scheme. This can work well for someone who is taking time out of the workforce or working in a reduced capacity, such as when starting a family or starting a business.

Here's an example of this in action:

- Your marginal tax rate when contributing to the scheme is 47 per cent, meaning the benefit to you of contributing is (marginal tax rate − 15 per cent) 32 per cent.
- Your marginal tax rate when withdrawing under FHSS is 19 per cent, meaning the tax applied on the withdrawal is (marginal tax rate − 30 per cent) 0 per cent.
- The result is that you end up saving 32 per cent tax on this money; based on total contributions of $50k this would be $16 000 in tax savings.

There's a strategic opportunity here if the stars align on your strategy.

As you can see, this strategy can help save you some tax dollars and get into the property market faster. You can also see that the rules are complex and it's not without risk. Given you're talking about some large numbers, take the time to understand the rules and consider getting some good professional advice before you rush in.

Different types of superannuation funds

Choosing the best super fund to hold your superannuation investments is one of the most important decisions you can make to get the most out of your super money.

There are four main types of super funds you should be aware of in order to make the right choice for you.

Industry funds

These are funds that were originally set up to service the workers within a specific industry. Most of these funds are not run for profit, which for many results in their fees being lower than the majority of other superannuation fund options.

Typical fees on an industry super fund are between 0.5 per cent and 1 per cent per annum, meaning that for every $100 000 you have invested you'll pay between $500 and $1000 every year.

Because industry funds are run as low-cost super products, generally speaking the available investment options are slightly more limited, and they typically don't invest as heavily in their technology, which can take away from your user experience.

These funds can be great at reducing your super fees, and many of them have decent investment options with good performance history.

Retail funds

Retail super funds are typically run by for-profit companies, and are generally more expensive than industry options, but most give access to a wider range of investment options.

Typical fees on retail super funds range between 0.5 per cent and a whopping 3 per cent, meaning that for every $100k you have invested the annual fees will be between $500 and $3000.

Corporate super funds

These types of funds are typically retail funds that are offered to larger employers with discounted pricing and sometimes even subsidised benefits like insurance cover. The super funds do this because they're chosen by the employer as the default superannuation option, meaning they get instant access to a large pool of potential members.

Typical fees on corporate super funds range between 0.5 per cent and 2 per cent, so for every $100k you have invested the annual fees will be between $500 and $2000.

Some of these corporate deals will also include ongoing financial education or access to an adviser, which can be helpful. Just keep in mind that if the source of your financial education is the provider of a financial product, there's a potential conflict of interest. It serves them for members to remain with their financial product.

Overall, how good a corporate super fund is depends on the deal an employer can strike with the provider. I've seen really good deals here with ultra-low fees and good subsidised benefits, and others that are very expensive without giving much in return. The devil is in the details, so if your employer offers a corporate fund you should take the time to understand how it compares with the alternatives.

Self-managed superannuation funds

Self-managed superannuation funds (SMSFs) are a special type of super fund that gives you full responsibility for the management of your superannuation money. With an SMSF your investment choice is essentially unlimited. You can use any sort of listed investment, from shares, ETFs or managed funds, to property, artwork, collectible cars—really anything of value.

But just because you can do something, it doesn't mean it's a good idea.

The operations of an SMSF are fairly involved and can be quite complicated and time consuming. When you start an SMSF, you essentially register the fund, set up a new tax file number, open up a bank account and investment accounts, and start investing your super money. Because it is its own tax entity, when you have an SMSF you need to complete a tax return for your fund each financial year. You also need to arrange an independent audit and annual registrations with the Australian Securities and Investments Commission (ASIC).

This ongoing work will generally cost you a minimum of $2500 each year, and if you have a lower super balance the fees as a percentage can be very high. Having more in your super can bring the cost down overall, and if you end up with a $1 million+ super fund, an SMSF can be significantly cheaper than some of the alternatives.

The big advantage of using an SMSF is that this sort of fund can buy residential property, and can borrow money from the bank to fund the purchase of a property just as if you were buying the property outside of super. This can allow you to use your super money to get into the property market, and essentially pay off a mortgage with pre-tax money through concessional super contributions.

That said, I believe most people should be looking to invest in property outside of superannuation, and the question then becomes 'Do you really need more property?' Also worth noting is that buying a property through an SMSF is an expensive exercise, with the initial costs generally being around $10k. There aren't a lot of banks that offer loans to SMSF borrowers, and the mortgage interest rates are typically 2 per cent higher than those you can access on a regular mortgage.

I've spoken with a lot of people considering using an SMSF because they want more control over how they invest their superannuation money. In reality, though, you can access most investments that people want (and that actually make sense for most people) through a cheaper option than using an SMSF.

How to choose a super fund

All these options have their benefits and disadvantages, and any option can be good for you and not so good for someone else. Unfortunately, there is no 'right' fund you should use or 'wrong' fund to avoid. But there's a right way to choose your super fund.

Start with your investments

Given your super fund is essentially just an investment account with more favourable tax rules, the investing strategy you follow with your super money will be the main driver of what super fund is best for you.

Through the work on investing you've done in the previous chapters, by now you should be clear on the investment strategy you want to follow moving forward. When you're trying to decide which super fund is best for you, you can narrow down the list of which funds make the most sense for you by starting with those that give you access to the investments you want.

Look at fees

Fees aren't everything when it comes to super, but they are important. Given that the super fund market is highly competitive and super fees are trending down over time, you should be looking at fees so you don't pay more than you have to.

Once you've narrowed down your potential super funds by looking at which give you access to the investments you want, you can rank the funds according to the sharpest pricing.

For example, if you want to follow an index fund passive investing approach, you could first look at the funds that offer good index investment options. From there, look at which ones are priced most competitively to get your shortlist.

Take advantage of comparison tools

These days there are a heap of comparison tools and websites that allow you to see how your super fund compares. You can compare fees, investment performance and features to gain a quick snapshot of your fund and give you ideas on some potential alternatives.

My favourite comparison tool is the ASIC MoneySmart superannuation comparison tool, which is provided by the Australian Government and doesn't have any advertising or promoted fund options.

When using these tools there are a couple of things to keep in mind. Be aware first that past performance doesn't guarantee future performance, particularly because the strategy or management of specific investment options can change over time. Also, keep in mind that superannuation is a long-term investment, meaning comparing over short time periods can be problematic. Instead, look at both the short- and long-term returns on the options you're comparing to get a more complete picture of how they stack up.

Look at features and user experience

Many super funds today offer a bunch of different bells and whistles with their funds. Some have slick apps, others offer you discounts on products and services, and still others have charitable giving programs built into their business operations.

If you value certain features or benefits in your super fund, such as the ability to buy exchange-traded funds (ETFs) or direct shares, better quality insurance cover or a slick user experience, you might be prepared to pay a little extra. But if you're paying for features you're not using, then your money is going to waste.

At the end of the day, your super fund is there to run the administration of your super investments, and while some of these benefits can be nice to have, I personally don't place a lot of value in the extra benefits you can get beyond having quality investments and good-value pricing.

That said, having a good technology back end can be helpful for you in keeping track of how your super is performing, and you can use this as a resource to educate yourself about investment markets and performance over time.

Understand what you want and what's available from your different super options, then you can compare the fees against funds with similar features.

Beware of insurance when switching

Many Aussies (young people in particular) fall into the trap of thinking they're bulletproof and don't need insurance, but research by the Australian Financial Services Council collected in their 'Underinsurance' report show we have a massive underinsurance gap in Australia. Having personally seen the huge difference good insurance can make to someone who needs it, I think insurance is an important part of being smart with your money.

Most super funds automatically give you a certain amount of life and disability insurance (and some income replacement cover) when you join. The details of insurance policies can get quite complex and there are some rules around what you can claim on a new policy vs one you've had for years, so tread carefully here.

If you don't think about your insurance cover when switching funds, you can end up losing the cover, which can be a serious problem if something goes wrong. If you're looking to switch your super, take the time to understand the insurance cover you have in place now, what's offered by the new fund, and what benefits you might be giving up if you switch. This way you can make an informed choice and make the right moves for you.

Don't set and forget

Once you've selected a quality super fund to deliver good investment performance over time, your work doesn't (quite) stop there.

Your super fund shouldn't need a lot of your time and attention, but the superannuation market is highly competitive and products tend to evolve (and get cheaper) over time.

This means that even if you've taken the time to compare and select the very best super fund for you today, you should check in again each year to give you confidence your fund is still your best choice.

THE WRAP

The fact that you can't access your super until you're old is an issue and not ideal, but this doesn't mean it should be ignored. The super tax rates are lower than every other option you have available for investing. And then there's the fact that a good chunk of your salary is going into your super, whether or not you choose to focus on it.

Superannuation is an investment vehicle that plays an important role on your journey to replace your salary by investing. Being smart with your super, getting your super investments working harder for you and using the rules to your advantage will help you get there faster.

It's common for people to ignore their super, putting it in the basket of 'something I'll only need to worry about in the future'. But a small amount of attention and focus earlier on your investing journey will pay big dividends over time.

Your action plan

- Do a super search through the ATO to get clear on where your super money is being held.

- Reread this chapter until you understand the key superannuation tax rules and how they can benefit you.

- Set your superannuation investment philosophy.

- Choose the best super fund for you, and consolidate your super (being careful of any insurance cover).

- Start making small, regular additional super contributions with a view to increasing these over time.

- Check in on your super fund at least once every three months to look at performance and how it's tracking.

- Do a formal comparison of your super every year to make sure it's still the best fund for you.

- Set a reminder to do a monthly one-minute check-in on your super fund to see how it's performing.

- Sit back and reap the rewards!

CHAPTER 7

Get tax smart

In Australia we pay a lot of tax, and tax is an area that causes a lot of uncertainty, confusion and frustration. When you aren't on top of your tax strategy, you pay more tax and have less money left over for investing (or spending), which reduces your forward momentum.

Tax is important because it pays for the things we need both as a country and as a society. But you shouldn't pay more tax than you have to. Every dollar of tax you save is an extra dollar you can use to replace your salary by investing faster, and to enjoy the journey a little more.

There are three main drivers of your rate of financial progress. The first is how much you spend and how much you save; the second is how much you invest; and the third is how much tax you pay.

Being smarter with tax, getting more out of what they have right now, is something everyone can do. But here's the thing: tax is something that's often hidden beneath the surface, because it's what happens *after* you buy and sell investments and *after* the financial year has ended. Because the rules are complicated and confusing, it's not always clear what's really driving your tax outcomes. This means it's easy for tax to go unnoticed, or to fall into the trap of thinking there's not a lot you can do to change your tax outcomes.

The good news is that there is a *heap* you can do to reduce your tax bill, *if* you know how to use the rules to your advantage. And luckily for you, you've made the (terrific) decision to buy this book! In this chapter I'm going to unpack the key things you need to know to make smarter moves with your tax, hold onto more of your income, and increase your after-tax investment returns to grow your investments and replace your salary faster.

Before we get into tax strategy there are some important things you need to know.

Your after-tax return is all that matters

To replace your salary by investing, by definition, over time you will build a substantial income stream from investments. All your investment returns are important, and the higher your investment return the faster you'll replace your salary.

But you should know that the *only* investment return that really matters is your *after-tax* return. This is how much you have left over *after* your ATO donation, which is the amount of money your investments will generate for you either to spend on your living expenses or to reinvest to continue growing your investments and wealth.

It's easy and common to focus on the headline return on your investments. While this return is important, it's not as important as your after-tax return.

You only get one tax rate

A common tax myth is that there are different taxes for different types of income, but this just isn't true.

Every person has only one taxable income and one tax scale that applies to that income. When you do your tax return, the ATO adds together all of your income from all sources, including your salary income, any overtime, bonus or commission income, interest income from bank accounts, dividend income from shares, and rental income from investment properties. This total income figure is called your 'assessable income'.

You then have tax deductions, which are also all added together to determine your total deductions. Your total deductions are subtracted from your total assessable income to determine your 'net assessable income'. This is the figure the ATO uses to establish how much tax you should pay.

If you are a salaried employee, your employer 'withholds' a certain amount of your income to cover the estimated tax you'll pay.

Side note: When you invest no one withholds any tax for you, meaning you're responsible for provisioning and preparing for any tax consequences of your investments (more on this later in the chapter).

When you complete a tax return, the ATO calculates the amount of your total tax payable. You then subtract any withheld tax to establish how much you'll receive as a tax refund, or if your tax bill is more than the amount of tax withheld you'll receive a tax bill.

Tax bills are a good thing

When people receive a tax bill for the first time they're often shocked and a little disappointed. But in reality, if you want to replace your salary by investing, receiving tax bills at some point should be expected. This is actually a good thing, because it means you've built a solid investment income. But don't get me wrong, we don't want your tax bill to be any higher than it absolutely needs to be.

Here's an example showing how this all fits together:

Salary income:	$100 000
Bank account interest:	5 000
Dividend income:	5 000
Net rental income from an investment property:	10 000
Total assessable income:	**120 000**
Less total deductions:	3000
Net assessable income:	**$117 000**

This is used to calculate total tax payable on net assessable income as per the current marginal tax rates less any tax withheld. This will drive your total tax refund, or tax payable.

In this example, you're taxed exactly the same amount as if you earned the $117 000 entirely from employment income, or from investment income, meaning there is no difference to the tax rate you pay on investment (or any other) income compared with your employment income.

Marginal tax rates

In Australia, we work under a marginal tax rate system, also known as a progressive tax system. The current marginal tax brackets (including full Medicare levy) are shown in table 7.1.

Table 7.1 Australian marginal tax brackets and rates

Taxable income	Tax on this income
0 – $18200	nil
$18201 – $45000*	21% for each dollar over $18200
$45001 – $120000	34.5% for each dollar over $45000 (plus tax from previous bracket)
$120001 – $180000	$29467 plus 39% for each dollar over $120000 (plus tax from previous brackets)
$180001 and over	$51667 plus 47% for each dollar over $180000 (plus tax from previous brackets)

*Medicare levy of 2% commences at $29033.

This table shows that as your income increases, so does the 'marginal rate' of tax you pay. One thing many people find confusing is that the higher marginal tax rates apply only to income earned above each threshold number. This means that even if your income is well into the top marginal tax bracket of $200000, you still pay no tax on the first $18200 of your income.

The implication is that if you're earning a salary and then start investing, any investment income is effectively added on top of your salary income and essentially 100 per cent of this income is taxed at your highest marginal tax rate. As this income grows, it may even push you into the next tax bracket and further increase your tax rate.

In some ways this is a good thing, because it means your investment income is increasing. But because marginal tax rates increase as your income increases, the more investment income you earn (or plan to earn) the more tax you're going to pay.

More is more when it comes to your income

When you receive a pay rise or bonus that raises total income into the next tax bracket, you may think this higher tax rate applies to your full income. This isn't the case. The higher marginal tax rate applies only to the amount of income earned within that particular tax bracket.

Also worth noting is that, excluding HECS and tax offsets, there's no point in the Australian tax system where you end up with less money after tax as a result of earning more income.

Value of deductions increases with your income

Nevertheless, the more you earn and the higher your marginal tax rate, the more of benefit every dollar of tax deductions will be to you. This means the more you earn, the more valuable it will be for you to maximise your deductions.

I'll unpack tax deductions and how to maximise them in detail later in the chapter.

Tax rates are different for different entities

To explain this concept, I'm going to need a little jargon (sorry). A *tax entity* is basically anything that has a tax file number (TFN) and that requires a tax return each year. For example, every individual taxpayer in Australia has a TFN and does (or should do) a tax return each year. This means every individual is their own tax entity. Every super fund, company and trust also has a TFN and again is its own tax entity.

I appreciate that companies and trusts might be foreign territory for many people, but they can be a powerful way to save you tax and protect your investments, so no matter where you're at with your money it's worth having at least a basic understanding of them and how they work.

Companies

The most common form of company in Australia is an operating business —
that is, an actual business that provides products or services. But companies
can also be used for investment purposes, and because companies have a
different tax rate from individuals this can create an opportunity to save tax.

Pretty much anyone can start a company, so long as you're not on a
government blacklist somewhere. You can do this pretty easily online or
with the help of a good accountant, and once you start a company you can
apply for a TFN. Once you have this, you can open up bank accounts and
investment accounts, and even buy property.

Investing through a company means that as opposed to holding the bank
account or investment in your personal name, it's held in the name of the
company and linked to the TFN of the company.

Then each year the company needs to do a tax return where investment
income is reported and taxed according to the company tax rules.
Companies are subject to a flat rate of tax of 30 per cent, which is lower
than the marginal tax rate an individual would pay on any income earned
above $45k per annum. This is where the tax-saving opportunity comes in
(more on that later).

Trusts

A trust is an entity for which special rules apply, the main one being that a
trust is required to distribute all income to another tax-paying entity, who
then pays tax on that income at their regular rate of tax. Trusts can distribute
income to individuals, but importantly they can also distribute income to
companies, which means the income is taxed at the company tax rate.

One big advantage of a trust is that it can change who income is distributed
to every single year. This means that in one year if you (or your partner)
have a lower income (when you're working less, say, around having a family

or starting a business) you can distribute it to one person. The next year, if incomes (and marginal tax rates) are higher you can distribute to someone else or to an investment company.

Table 7.2 gives a breakdown of the different rates of tax that apply to different tax-paying entities.

Table 7.2 Tax rates across different tax entities

	Individual	Superfund	Company	Trust
Tax rate	Income—MTR 39% Capital gains—MTR with 50% discount available	Income—15% Capital gains—15% with discount available to 10%	Income—30% Capital gains—30% (no discount)	Variable based on where income is 'distributed'

When you're in the process of growing your wealth through investing, you're generally moving new capital each year into your investments, which in turn generates investment income. Each year you pay tax on this income, then reinvest what's left to continue growing your investments and wealth.

The implication is that the less tax you pay, the more money you have left over to reinvest, and the faster your investments will grow. This means there's an opportunity to be strategic with *where* you invest, an opportunity that can make a significant difference to your wealth trajectory.

For example, the maximum tax rate that applies to a company is 30 per cent—significantly lower than the top marginal tax rate of 47 per cent. If you're already earning a good income that puts you into one of the higher marginal tax brackets, if you want to replace your salary by investing and do it all in your personal name, eventually you're going to be pushed into the top marginal tax bracket, where every dollar of investment income earned will be taxed at 47 per cent.

In comparison, when growing your investments under a company structure, investment income would have tax applied at a maximum rate of 30 per cent. The result is you hold onto an additional 17 per cent of your investment income that you can then reinvest to grow your investments faster. With superannuation it gets even better, as the maximum tax rate that applies to investment income earned through superannuation is 15 per cent.

Table 7.3 shows an example of the tax that would apply to investment income at different levels.

Table 7.3 Taxing investment income

Investment income p.a.	$50 000	$100 000	$150 000	$200 000
[individual] tax at 47%	$23 500	$47 000	$70 500	$84 000
[company] tax at 30%	$15 000	$30 000	$45 000	$60 000
[company] tax saving (annual)	$8500	$17 000	$25 500	$34 000
[super] tax at 15%	$7500	$15 000	$22 500	$30 000
[super] tax saving (annual)	$16 000	$32 000	$48 000	$54 000

As you can see from these figures, the potential tax savings could be in the tens of thousands of dollars every single year. But the rules are complicated and confusing, and there are risks and downsides to consider.

Firstly, there are costs involved with setting up tax entities such as investment companies and trusts, as well as ongoing tax return and administration costs each year. For tax entities to benefit you, they need to give you tax savings or other benefits in excess of the amount of extra money you pay.

Then there's the fact that companies don't receive long-term investing capital gains discount, the land tax implications of using trusts, the implications of locking your money away in superannuation, and the time and admin needed to manage a more complicated investment portfolio. These strategies aren't for everyone, but if you have big financial goals, it's worth considering trusts and companies when you invest.

If you're thinking about taking this sort of approach, I strongly suggest that you be prepared to invest in some good professional advice before you jump in.

Tax planning across family units is valuable

As we've just covered, different tax rates apply to different individuals and tax entities. This is one of the main areas of opportunity for your tax planning. Being strategic with where you own your investments can drastically change your after-tax return.

Table 7.4 gives an example of the tax rates available for a family and the different tax structures and tax rates they could use to invest.

Table 7.4 Tax planning across a family group

	Mum earning $125k	Dad earning $35k	15-year-old daughter earning $1500	18-year-old daughter earning $10k	Superfund	Company	Trust
Tax rate	Income— MTR* 39% Capital gains— MTR with 50% discount available	Income— MTR 21% Capital gains— MTR with 50% discount available	Income— MTR 47%** Capital gains— MTR with 50% discount available	Income— MTR 0% Capital gains— MTR with 50% discount available	Income— 15% Capital gains— 15% with discount available to 10%	Income— 30% Capital gains—30% (no discount)	Variable based on where income is 'distributed'
Tax payable based on investment income of $10k	$3900	$2100	$4700	$0	$1500	$3000	n/a

*MTR = marginal tax rate
**Minors are taxed on investment income at a higher rate than adult taxpayers

You can see from the above, that the difference between paying tax at the highest rate (and therefore the potential tax saving) across these groups compared with the lowest is $4700, which is money you could use to grow your investments faster.

My five most effective tax-saving strategies

As the end of each financial year rolls around I get a lot of people reaching out thinking about the looming EOFY deadline and what can be done to reduce their impending tax bill.

The reality is that what you can do in the last days of the financial year is somewhat limited. The best time to start being smart with your tax is the first day of the financial year, and there are some strategies that can seriously improve your tax position for the financial year ahead.

Here I unpack my top five tax-saving strategies and the key things you should focus on throughout each financial year to set yourself up for the best possible outcomes once the financial year is done and dusted.

Franked dividend share investing

Buying shares gives you a small piece of ownership in a company, and through this ownership you benefit from the growth in value of the company and receive part of any profits paid through dividends.

In Australia, most companies pay tax on their profits *before* paying dividends to shareholders. The ATO are kind enough not to tax this income twice, so when a dividend is paid by a company from their after-tax profit you receive a tax credit for the tax already paid on the dividend income. These tax credits are referred to as 'franking credits'.

This can seem confusing, but in reality it's pretty simple. When profits are paid out to shareholders through dividends, the tax that's already been paid on the profits is recorded. Then, when you submit your tax return and include your dividend income, the tax already paid counts to reduce the amount of tax you owe.

In short, the impact of franked dividends on your tax position is the difference between your tax rate and the tax rate paid by the company paying your dividends. This can be a positive or negative difference, so you can owe tax or tax can be owed to you.

For example, if your current marginal tax rate is 39 per cent (income above $120 000 p.a.) and the tax on your dividends was paid at the company tax rate of 30 per cent, you will need to pay only the difference of 9 per cent tax. Not bad, but it can get even better ...

If your tax rate is 19 per cent (that is, you're earning income up to $45 000 p.a.) and again tax has been paid at 30 per cent, you actually receive a tax *refund* on your dividends of 11 per cent. This amount is paid in cash as part of your tax refund.

Franking credits have a big impact on the after-tax return on your investments and can save you thousands of dollars every year, helping you to save tax *and* grow your investments faster. And their impact can be significant.

Here's an example showing the difference between having your investment income made up of franked dividends vs unfranked dividends, assuming your aim is to replace the average Australian annual pre-tax salary of $92 029. The tax that would apply on this level of income in the current financial year (FY22–23) tax rates is $22 247, meaning the net after-tax income is $69 782.

If you were looking to replace this level of income with investment income that doesn't come with franking credits attached, you'd need to replace the full amount of $92 029 then pay tax at marginal rates, to be left with $69 782 after tax.

But if you were to build dividend income that was fully franked, with tax paid at the company tax rate of 30 per cent, you'd need to receive dividends of only $64 421, which would come with attached tax credits of $27 609. The result is you'd end up with the same amount of income after tax but need less headline income (and therefore wealth) to get there.

For the engineers, teachers and other analytical types out there, the working on this is as follows:

Franking credit
= (dividend amount / (1 – company tax rate)) – dividend amount.

Or:

Franking credit [$27 609]
= (dividend amount [$64 421] / (1 – company tax rate[30%]))
– dividend amount [$64 421].

The implication of this, going back to our initial investment income assumption of 5 per cent, is that you can have less in your investment portfolio to generate the same level of income.

To generate an after-tax income of $64 421, assuming a 5 per cent income rate, if this income was made up entirely of fully franked dividends you'd need investments worth $1 288 420. If, on the other hand, this income is made up of regular (unfranked) dividends or other investment income without franking credits attached, you'd instead need to have total investments of $1 840 580, assuming the same 5 per cent rate of return.

This shows you can have $552 160 *less* in your investment portfolio and receive the same level of income, meaning you're just as 'wealthy' but with less wealth. This shows the power of smart tax planning.

A note on risk: I should call out that this is a fairly simple example, and there are a number of considerations when it comes to building wealth, not least of these diversification.

While Australian shares are great, the Aussie share market is small relative to the rest of the world. Concentrating your investments in one country comes with risk.

Every money option comes with benefits and downsides. The key to making the smartest moves for you is understanding your risks and which ones are right for you.

Debt recycling

This is probably my top go-to strategy for homeowners looking to pay down their mortgage and build investments tax effectively at the same time. Debt recycling is the process of replacing non-deductible mortgage debt (like your home mortgage), with tax-deductible investment debt.

Essentially, how debt recycling works is that you make extra payments on your mortgage, and move the same amount of your extra payments into an investment (generally a share portfolio). This strategy centres on the fact that instead of just investing money from your bank account directly into shares, you take this money from another loan facility that's set up solely for the purpose of investing.

The rules can get a little complex and confusing here, but the strategy works because you're paying down your home loan (non-tax-deductible) debt, and at the same time drawing money from a separate loan for the purpose of investing, which makes the interest repayments on this loan tax deductible.

Debt recycling in action

Here's a practical example showing debt recycling in action. In this example, you have a home mortgage of $500 000 against a property value of $1 million, and have a spare $500 per week you want to use to save/invest/get ahead.

To set up a debt-recycling strategy, the first step is to speak to your bank or mortgage broker to set up a new loan. This loan is generally secured against your property, and would essentially sit there with funds available ready for you to draw against.

In week 1 of the strategy, you pay your spare $500 as an extra payment on your mortgage (table 7.5). At the same time you withdraw the same $500 amount from the new loan set up for investment purposes and invest this money in a share portfolio.

Table 7.5 Debt recycling in action 1

	Day 0	Day 7	Day 365	Day 3650 (year 10 of strategy)
Total home (non-deductible) debt	$500 000	$499 500	$474 000	$240 000
Total investment (deductible) debt	$0	$500	$26 000	$260 000
Total debt	$500 000	$500 000	$500 000	$500 000

Note that because this strategy revolves around paying down non-tax-deductible mortgage debt, it's really only viable for people who have a mortgage against their home or another property that's not an investment (and therefore not already tax deductible).

In table 7.6 (overleaf) I build on our previous example to show the interest deductions you can create and the potential tax you can save. For this example I use a marginal tax rate of 34.5 per cent, which is the tax rate (including Medicare levy) you'd pay if your annual taxable income is above $45 000.

Table 7.6 Debt recycling in action 2

	At end of year 1	At end of year 10	At end of year 20
Total home (non-deductible) debt	$474 000	$240 000	$0
(Non-deductible) interest @ 5%	$23 700	$12 000	$0
Total investment (deductible) debt	$26 000	$260 000	$500 000
(Deductible) interest @ 5%	$1300 p.a.	$13 000 p.a.	$25 000 p.a.
Tax refund @ 39%	$507 p.a.	$5070 p.a.	$9750 p.a.
Total debt	$500 000	$500 000	$500 000

One benefit of debt recycling is that over time you're 'recycling' non-tax-deductible mortgage debt and essentially turning it into tax-deductible investment debt, increasing your tax deductions and reducing the amount of tax you pay. Through this strategy, your debt levels remain *exactly the same*; what changes is the proportion of your debt that's tax deductible.

If you're investing and have a mortgage, you could choose to invest the money directly into your investment account (that is, not through a debt facility as part of a debt-recycling strategy) and not get the tax deductions. Or you could choose to do exactly the same level of investing, and boost your tax deductions and cut your tax bill in the process.

There are very few 'no-brainers' when it comes to your money, but this is one of them.

The other main benefit of this strategy comes from the fact that the long-term return on shares (9.8 per cent) is higher than the long-term average mortgage interest rates. This will lead to your share portfolio growing at a faster rate than the interest you pay on your investment debt. Eventually you can sell down your shares, and you should have enough money to clear your debt *and* have money left over.

What are the risks of debt recycling?

The first key risk or downside of following a debt-recycling strategy is that you don't actually reduce your debt levels over time. This is because you're increasing tax-deductible debt while reducing your non-tax-deductible debt. Increasing your deductible debt is clearly a positive, but the net result is that your debt levels don't actually reduce.

Carrying more debt means risk around increasing interest rates, the cashflow risk of having to fund your debt repayments, and the potential negative impact if you lose your job or want to change careers or roles.

To minimise this risk, take the time to put together a clear exit plan for your debt, build up a solid cash buffer for emergencies, and think about insurance such as income replacement cover to reduce the risk of the unexpected.

You will also face some risk with this strategy driven by the fact that you're going to be investing money into the share market, which can be volatile.

When there is disruption in the economy or the share market, often even the best companies will suffer a drop in their share price. This means your share portfolio can end up being worth less than the amount of money you've invested. And because with debt recycling you're essentially using borrowed money, you might be in a position where you owe more than the value of your investments at a point in time.

It's critical in this case that you have a solid plan in place and choose good investments that will bounce back when markets recover, and that you put yourself in a position where you're not forced to sell your investments at the wrong time.

Superannuation contributions

Under the current super rules, you can add up to $27500 to your superannuation every year and claim a tax deduction. This amount includes the money put in by your employer, but for most people this still leaves room for a pretty chunky tax deduction.

For people with super fund balances below $500000, you can also 'catch up' on your unused contributions from previous years, contributing up to five years' worth of your unused contribution cap amount in one year.

Once money is invested through super it's subject to concessional tax rates of no more than 15 per cent, which is generally much lower than your marginal tax rates, further helping your investments grow faster.

The deductions available for contributing to super, combined with the lower rate of tax on investments held within a superannuation fund, make this strategy worth including in your investing game plan.

Super can also be used throughout your journey to replace your salary by investing, particularly when you're selling larger investments like property. Given this is something everyone will likely do at some point in their investing journey, I'll unpack how it works with an example.

Selling a property

Selling a property often results in a chunky cash injection, which if managed well can be a huge accelerator of your wealth building. With property, given the size of the numbers, the difference between doing it well and just doing it can be huge, so making the smartest steps will pay big dividends here.

Based on the long-term Australian property growth rate of 6.3 per cent, if you'd bought an 'average' property as an investment in Sydney in 2011, when the median house price was $634000, 11 years later you could sell that property for $1265517—netting you a total capital gain of $631517.

But what happens *after* you sell is crucial.

A couple earning the average income in Australia of $92 029 would each pay tax on that income of $22 247. Based on a total gain of $631 517 and the current tax rules, because they've held the investment for longer than 12 months a 50 per cent discount applies to their capital gain, to bring this down to $315 758. Assuming the property is held in their joint names, we split the gain again to a total taxable capital gain of $157 879 per person.

This amount would then be added to your other income of $92 029, bringing your ATO assessable income to $249 908. The total tax per person would be $88 154, or $176 308 in total tax for the couple.

You'd still end up with a solid amount of money after paying your tax, and most people would be happy with this as an outcome. But it could be much better…

Every taxpayer has the ability to make tax-deductible contributions to super. These contributions reduce your ATO assessable income and therefore how much tax you pay.

If you're earning $92 029, your employer would be making compulsory super guarantee contributions of $9663. But the limit for concessional super contributions is $27 500, meaning you have room to make another $17 837 in tax-deductible contributions in the current financial year.

For our couple, contributing at this level would reduce their taxable income to $232 071 and mean their personal tax bill would be $79 770, a reduction of $8384 per person or $16 768 combined.

But it can get even better…

A few years back the government introduced 'catch-up' super contributions. If you have less than $500 000 in your super fund and you haven't contributed up to your full concessional contribution limit in financial years since the 2018–19 financial year, you can catch up on these contributions in the current financial year.

This means that for someone who has been receiving super contributions of $9663 each year for the past five financial years, the total 'unused' contributions are $81 685. (For the engineers following along at home, the limit was increased from $25 000 to $27 500 in the 2021/22 financial year, which makes the calculation a little more complicated.)

Going back to our couple, if they were to each contribute $81685 to their super funds in the current financial year, their total tax payable would reduce to $50074 per person, or $100148 combined.

Comparing this with our starting tax position of $176308, this reflects a total personal tax saving of $76160 for our couple. A serious amount of extra cash that can be directed to wealth building or other money goals. This example highlights the difference between good and great when it comes to your tax planning.

Borrowing to buy shares

This one isn't for everyone and definitely comes with some risk that must be managed, but it can be an effective way to get some tax deductions and grow your wealth at the same time.

Given the long-term expected return on Australian shares of 9.8 per cent is generally higher than borrowing interest rates, borrowing money and investing in shares should provide you with a net benefit after paying your borrowing costs. And it gets better...

Because interest costs on debt used for the sole purpose of investing is tax deductible, the after-tax cost of your borrowing is actually lower than the headline interest rate you pay.

I'm not a fan of margin loans, which I think come with a considerable amount of risk *and* a high interest rate, along with the risk of margin calls. Where I see this strategy work well is when you own property that has enough equity to borrow against. This way you can borrow at close to standard mortgage interest rates, meaning your investments need to do less work for the strategy to benefit you.

Borrowing to invest can seriously accelerate your returns, but it can also amplify your losses. If you're thinking about going down this path it's critical you have a solid plan and risk management strategy in place, and think about getting some good professional advice before you jump in.

Negative gearing

Investing in Australia comes with some serious tax perks, where you can claim a tax deduction for the costs of borrowing money to invest, which is most commonly done with property investments. This can help you invest more *and* cut your tax bill at the same time, and is one of my favourite tax-saving and wealth-building strategies.

Refer back to the full negative gearing explainer and an example of how it works in practice in chapter 4. When you're investing or just planning out your future investments, you should take the time to understand the negative gearing rules and how to use them to your advantage.

Maximise your deductions and tax return

When most people consider tax planning, the first thing they think about is how to pump up their tax refund. While this is valuable and shouldn't be ignored, the strategies and tactics I've outlined are much more powerful than finding an extra couple of hundred dollars in things to claim on your tax return.

That said, every dollar of tax you can save is an extra dollar you can use to replace your salary by investing, so it should absolutely be part of your tax planning. I'll now outline the key areas you should be aware of to get the most out of your tax return.

Understand your potential deductions

In Australia there's a laundry list of expenses you're able to claim as tax deductions. Among the most common are:

- self-education expenses
- premiums for income replacement insurance
- cost of professional tax advice and investment advice
- home office expenses
- work-related travel expenses
- interest costs on investment debt
- investment-related fees and expenses.

These deductions are common no matter what your occupation, but there are also a number of specific deductions that are based on specific occupations. The full list can be found on the ATO website, and educating yourself on what tax deductions you can claim and what you can't will pay off here.

The most overlooked tax deductions I see are around self-education and professional development, which can often run into thousands of dollars of tax deductions every year. Recent data from social researcher McCrindle shows 30 per cent of Aussies spend an average of $1936 on professional education each year.

The ATO has clarified that any self-education expenses that increase your income-earning potential are deductible, which applies even where they're in an area outside your direct line of work. For example, if I was to purchase an online cooking class that helps me learn how to structure an online course on investing, there's an indirect link to my income that would likely satisfy the ATO's criteria for deductibility.

You can also generally deduct the cost of content subscriptions that help with your work, like newspaper or online news site subscriptions. This means that along with formal study, any short courses, online training or other content-based education can help to cut your tax bill.

Bring forward (necessary) purchases

If you're spending on things that are deductible, incurring the expense in June as the last month of the financial year compared with in July, the first month of the new financial year, will mean you receive the tax benefits a full year earlier.

Spending on something that's tax deductible will save you tax, and it makes a lot of sense to bring forward your tax-deductible spending before EOFY. But deductible expenses do still cost you money even after the tax saving. This means spending before EOFY will put you in a better position only if these expenses are things you really *need*.

Sell investments in a loss position

When you sell an investment for less than you paid for it you lock in a 'capital loss' that's reported to the ATO. These losses then offset any capital gains you have in the same financial year.

If you've made investment gains within a financial year and have investments in a loss position, selling them before the end of the financial year will reduce your investment tax bill.

The ATO stipulates that you can't sell investments just to claim a loss then repurchase them—this is called a 'wash sale' and is a big no-no. But it's common and completely reasonable for you to review your portfolio before EOFY with a view to exiting underperforming investments, and this in turn creates an opportunity for tax savings.

To assess if this will benefit you, look at your investments through the current financial year and confirm any gains you've made. Then look at any investments you have in a loss position with a view to balancing out your gains.

Be aware that investment losses don't help to reduce non-investment income, so unfortunately they can't reduce tax on your employment income. But given the ups and downs we've seen in investment markets in recent financial years, selling down investments at a loss might make a big difference to your tax position.

Prepay deductible interest

When you borrow money for investment purposes, the interest costs on this debt are tax deductible in the financial year they are paid. This means if you prepay your interest costs before EOFY, you can boost your deductions and increase your tax return.

Get good professional advice

Most people know that your accountant's fees are deductible, but don't realise that fees paid for investment and strategic tax advice are also generally tax deductible when they relate to building your investment income.

This advice can help you build your investments and wealth faster, and getting a deduction for the cost of the advice amplifies the benefit to you.

Keep good records

It's worth emphasising that it's critical you keep good records of your deductible expenses if you want to claim them. I talk to too many people who aren't on top of their record keeping through the tax year, only to realise when doing their tax returns that they don't have the information they need to claim their deductions.

Setting up a digital tax shoebox and staying on top of your record keeping through the financial year will make your life easier at tax time and mean you can claim everything you're entitled to.

Who helps with your tax planning?

Getting good help with your tax can be harder than it should be. In the past, tax planning was the sole responsibility of your personal accountant, who would help you understand all the rules and how to use them to your advantage.

But the personal accounting market has changed. With changes to how businesses operate and the significant increases in costs to accounting firms, personal income tax returns are no longer a very profitable business activity.

This surprises most people, but when you think it through it makes a lot of sense. An accountant will generally charge a few hundred dollars for a tax return, and even that can seem expensive to the person paying the bill. Meanwhile, the typical hourly rate for a good accountant is somewhere between $300 and $1000 an hour.

This means that if an accountant is charging you a few hundred dollars they can afford to spend only a short time with you if they don't want to lose money on this work. Any good accounting company will rely heavily on technology and processes around their client data collection to minimise the time spent with each individual.

Personal tax returns are a volume game, and the unfortunate consequence for you is that because your accountant *needs* to minimise the time spent with you, it's unlikely you're going to get the nurturing guidance and education that many of the people I speak to would like from a relationship with their tax adviser.

This means you'll need to do part of the heavy lifting around your tax planning either yourself, or with support other than from your accountant.

The ideas covered in this chapter should be a good starting point for building your knowledge around tax strategies and planning, and in the next chapter on your game plan I'll cover how you can bake smart tax decisions into your money strategy moving forward.

But as your situation becomes more complex over time, and the impact of your money moves gets larger, you should consider bringing in some extra support to help you make the very best decisions for you. Any good financial adviser who helps people in the 'wealth accumulation' space will be well versed on tax planning and strategy, and bringing in this sort of support early can help you accelerate your progress.

Because most advice fees for investment building and tax planning are also tax deductible, this can help you get some smart advice and cut your tax bill at the same time.

THE WRAP

The opportunities and financial benefits you can get from smart tax planning are substantial and shouldn't be ignored.

Trying to build wealth without considered and strategic tax planning is like trying to drive a car with the handbrake on. It can be done, but your progress will be slow and you'll never reach the speed you otherwise could.

Every dollar of tax you save is an extra dollar you can put to work for you, so take the time to understand the tax rules and how to use them to your advantage. This way you'll hold onto more of your income and get ahead faster and easier.

Warning: In this chapter, I've outlined and unpacked some strategies that could save you significant amounts of tax. I've done my best to explain them in enough detail to help you understand what's important, but in as simple a way as possible. Please note that these strategies are complex, and there are nuanced rules and risks that are important for anyone considering using these strategies to understand.

The last thing I would want is for you to rush into something without having all the knowledge you need to make the very best decisions possible for you. This is not tax advice, and I strongly suggest you seek out and invest in some quality financial and tax advice before implementing any of these strategies. Even if you have to pay $20k for this advice (and you won't), given the potential tax savings this would pay for itself multiple times over.

So please note that this is not just the standard legal disclaimer I have to make. it's my sincere, heartfelt warning, because I want to make sure you get the best results and avoid making mistakes you'll regret.

Your action plan

- [ ] Read and reread the start of this chapter until you understand the marginal tax rate rules and their impact when you invest.

- [ ] Get clear that your *after-tax* investment return is the only one that actually matters.

- [ ] Consider where is best for you to own your investments—whether in your personal name(s), super or other tax entities.

- [ ] Take the time to understand my top five tax-saving strategies as explained in this chapter.

- [ ] Understand the deductions you can claim and those you can't.

- [ ] Start your tax planning at the *start* of the financial year, not the end.

- [ ] Engage someone (or multiple someones) to help with your tax planning and strategy as your situation evolves over time.

CHAPTER 8

Your game plan

A few years back a couple came to me in an okay financial position, but after I got to know them and their background better I found out they'd made a major mistake that cost them hundreds of thousands of dollars.

Through their late 20s and early 30s they had saved hard to buy their first home. They bought a lovely terrace home in Five Dock in Sydney's inner west. The property wasn't cheap but it wasn't extravagant, and they loved it.

When they were planning the purchase they did all of the things you're told to do, and thought they were set up for success. But they missed one big thing that came back to bite them a few years later.

When purchasing the property, they took the time to make sure it fitted with their budget, and they included a bit of a buffer to cover increases in mortgage interest rates. At the time they figured this was important to ensure the purchase would work well for them.

After the purchase things were going well, they lived a good life and the property started increasing in value. They got married and started planning a family. This is when they realised they were headed for financial trouble.

When they started looking at the financial impact around maternity and paternity leave, returning to work initially in a part-time capacity, and including day-care costs, their budget just wasn't adding up. They couldn't do all the things they wanted around starting a family *and* live the lifestyle they wanted *and* afford the mortgage repayments on their home. Something had to give.

They tried tweaking some of the numbers but realised the sacrifices were greater than they were prepared to make. Ultimately they decided they needed to sell their home.

They sold the property around three years after they'd purchased it, and made around $300k after all their expenses. Good money no doubt, but the potential was so much greater...

I helped them plan and execute the purchase of another property to get them back on the property ladder around four years after they had sold their first home. But in that four-year period, the property market in Sydney had increased significantly and they ended up getting a lot less for the same money they'd sold their first place for.

This is an example of a situation in which you can make an investment that makes you a bunch of money but ends up being the wrong move for you.

If they'd spent a little less on the property, or purchased the property as an investment and rented the place they wanted to live in, they would have been able to hold the property for the long term, and benefited so much more, both financially and personally, from the purchase.

If you ask yourself whether a property is a good investment in absolute terms, but not whether it's the right investment for *you*, it can be a disaster.

In this chapter I want to help you figure out how to build *your* ideal plan to replace your salary by investing so you can avoid problems like this and fast-track your progress.

A typical replace your salary journey

While there's only one set of steps that will work for you to replace your salary by investing, there is a broad common pathway everyone will follow.

By now some of this should feel a little obvious, but there are a few things to look out for that will make your life easier. And, before we bring it all together in your game plan I want to make sure you're crystal clear on what's what.

Stage 1: Growing your assets

The first stage of your wealth-building journey is—you guessed it—building your investments and wealth. The goal of replacing your salary can only be achieved once you have enough assets to provide you with your ideal investment income. This means that in the early stages of your journey your primary focus should be on building assets.

You should note there will be a different strategy once you're getting closer to living off your investment income. This distinction is an important one, because the strategies that are best to grow your assets *aren't* exactly the same as those that are best to grow your income.

When you're focusing on growing your assets, leverage (borrowing) is your friend. In fact, it's the strategy that will make the biggest difference to how quickly your investments grow. But be aware that running high debt levels is probably not where you want to be once you're relying on your investments to pay your salary.

Getting started investing

The first step in building your assets is to start investing. Most commonly, this is done with share investing (or ETFs, micro-investing or similar), where you can start with a small amount and build your assets through regular investment contributions.

As your money momentum starts to build and accelerate, the next big step is property, where you'll start introducing the power of leverage to your investing and wealth building.

Enter the property market

As covered in chapter 4, your first property investment is most likely not going to be your first home, so you should look at it as an investment transaction rather than this huge emotional purchase.

As you get closer to buying your investment property, unless you're doing this with a family guarantee, you'll want to start building the cash savings to fund your deposit. At this point you might reduce your regular investing, or even sell down your ETFs or shares, to hold your property deposit in cash where it's protected from the share market's ups and downs.

After you've worked through the previous chapter on tax, I hope you now recognise the importance and power of smart tax planning. I strongly recommend you prepare a full, end-to-end tax plan *before* you buy your first property, as well as before each future property. This will help you optimise your tax structuring and decision making to deliver the best *after-tax* return.

Once you buy a property, you can reset your planning, set your sights on your next big move then switch your focus back to building assets through share investing. It's also good practice to review and revisit your tax planning as needed before you make the shift from one investment focus to another.

This is the key to the asset-building stage of your replace your salary by investing journey. Don't get me wrong, it sounds simple—but that doesn't mean it's easy!

Through this process you'll be making big decisions, and the difference between *good* and *great* is likely to be measured in the hundreds of thousands of dollars, so you'll want to take the time to get your approach right.

How much cash do you need?

As noted in chapter 3, it's important that when you invest you can cover all the other spending that's important to you, and that you have cash savings to fall back on (your emergency fund). This way you won't be forced to sell investments at a time that doesn't make sense and lose money as a result.

At the same time, you want to hold as little cash as possible at any given time, because the long-term return on cash is much lower than the long-term return on almost every other investment out there. This means that as you progress you should aim to invest any cash that isn't needed for your upcoming expenses, your larger investments (such as buying property) and your emergency fund.

As you set your sights on buying your first and subsequent properties, this will change. At that time, cash isn't just sitting there not working for you; it's giving you the option to buy a great property that's going to help you accelerate your wealth building.

In the really early stages of your journey to replace your salary by investing you'll likely have fewer financial commitments and lower financial risk, so your emergency fund can be smaller. Over time, as your commitments grow, you'll want to increase your emergency fund. The 'right' amount is driven by the actual risks for you and how you feel about those risks, but clearly a 21-year-old who still lives at home will need less in an emergency fund than a 40-year-old with two kids and three investment properties.

Buying your dream home

Owning your dream home is an important part of true money success, and something that's achievable for everyone who's prepared to put in the work to make it happen. That said, it's important your dream is realistic given the financial position you're in, and specifically that your spend on your dream home is consistent with the financial trajectory you're on and the other assets and investments you have in place.

Careful and considered planning is your friend here, and the more you spend on your dream home, the more important this planning is. When planning your dream home purchase, you need to make sure you're able to pay off any mortgage on this property in a timeframe you're happy with *and* live the lifestyle you want *and* still build your investment assets at the rate you need to get where you want to be *when* you want to be there.

If you buy your dream home at the wrong time on your journey, you'll seriously slow your financial progress. Timing is everything.

As mentioned in chapter 4, it is useful to see your dream home purchase as an expense rather than an investment, because while you live in your dream home it won't actually make you any real money. In fact, running a mortgage on your own home will cost you money.

So when you're planning your dream home you need to make sure it fits with all the other things you want to do with your money. If the numbers don't stack up, it means that now isn't the right time to buy it. I get that this is frustrating, because we want it all now. We work hard, take our money seriously and are polite to strangers, so surely we *deserve* our dream home. But I never said real financial success was easily (or quickly) accomplished.

If now isn't the time to buy your dream home, all is not lost. It's an opportunity for you to focus instead on growing your wealth, and it's likely you'll be able to accelerate your progress here without a huge mortgage or tying up a big chunk of your money. You can then refocus and reset your targets with a view to buying your dream home once the numbers add up.

Stage 2: Transition to income

The next stage of your journey to replace your salary by investing commonly has two main features. You will often pull back on your formal work commitments, and your regular salary income will reduce as you replace this with investment income. The second important element is that you start structuring your assets to maximise the income they're delivering to your bank account.

When you're in the process of growing your assets, you'll likely have higher debt levels and a bigger proportion of your total assets allocated to property. This investment mix is ideal when you're growing your wealth, but when it comes to your income there are two issues with this approach.

Firstly, servicing ongoing mortgage repayments drains your cashflow and increases your living expenses. This means you'll need more investments to generate more income, which can mean it takes much longer to get to the point of being able to replace your salary by investing.

Secondly, property isn't as good as shares when it comes to generating an investment income, because a larger proportion of the total return on property investments is tied up in the growth in the value of a property.

As a reminder from the previous chapters, the long-term total return on property vs shares is fairly similar, at 8.66 per cent for property and 9.8 per cent for shares. The difference comes from how these returns are made up. With property, the total return is made up of 6.3 per cent growth return (increase in property value over time) and 2.33 per cent net rental income return (after all ongoing property costs). With shares, the return is broken down as 5.4 per cent growth return (increase in value of shares over time) and 4.4 per cent income (from dividends).

You can see from these figures that the income return on shares is around double that of property. Putting these numbers into context, $2 million in property assets would deliver you an annual income of around $46 000, whereas $2 million in shares would deliver you an annual income of around $88 000.

But there's a further advantage with shares, because a share (or ETF or managed fund, for example) will typically have a price somewhere between $10 and $200, meaning that if the dividend income alone isn't enough to give you the salary you want, you can sell a share to realise some extra cash. When you own a property, you can't just sell off one bedroom if you need some extra cash. Property is a lumpy asset with large buy and sell costs.

Selling properties to boost your investment income

If you're fortunate enough to find yourself in a strong wealth position, you may choose to hold onto one or more investment properties even after you achieve financial freedom. If you can find a way to keep properties and even keep running debt, *and* at the same time have enough assets to generate your ideal salary, this is a good thing. It will likely mean your asset position will continue to grow over time, even though you're not necessarily adding more new money to your investments.

But for most people, and for anyone who wants to achieve financial freedom as quickly as possible, it's likely you'll need to restructure your investments to focus on income. Specifically, you'll most likely need to sell down investment properties and rebalance this money in investments such as shares either inside or outside of superannuation.

I hate to be the bearer of bad news, but unfortunately selling investment properties will mean you'll need to pay some capital gains tax. While we never feel great about paying tax, this is the cost of doing business and simply means you've made some good money from your investment.

That said, there are a number of strategies and tactics you can use to minimise the amount of tax you pay when you sell a property. The first concerns how you structure your property investment in the first place, whether you own the property personally or in joint names, or through a trust, company or superannuation fund. Revisit chapter 7 if you need a refresher on tax.

When the time comes to sell your property the horse will have well and truly bolted here, which is why it's critical you think through the long-term tax implications of a property purchase *before* you buy.

Understanding your options to reduce tax as you sell down and restructure your investments will make a significant difference to your *after-tax* investing profit. The rules are complex and can be confusing; the implications are long lasting, and you really get only one shot at getting this right. In my completely biased view as a financial planner, this is another one of those times you should definitely look at finding some quality financial advice to get the best possible outcomes for you.

Pathways to 'retirement'

There are two common pathways to 'retirement' that will dictate the best way to transition your investments from a growth focus to an income focus. Please note that when I talk about retirement, I'm not necessarily talking about pulling up stumps and becoming a full-time bingo player or lawn bowls pro. What I mean is that your money is set up in such a way that you no longer *need* to work and earn a pay cheque.

At that point, if you choose to continue to work because you want to, great. If you instead choose to travel or take extended leave to spend more time with your family, also great. Or if you choose to spend your time volunteering on a cause that's important to you, all the better. The key is that you get to choose what you allocate your time to instead of needing to work for a salary to cover your living expenses or further build your investments.

Back to our pathways to 'retirement'. Some people work in a job that lends itself to the option of working part time. They will likely go through a stage when they have some income coming in, but it's less than they would be earning if they were still working full time. Some regular income can be helpful in allowing you to spend less of your investment income and have more you can channel into building wealth.

Others will choose to exit paid employment fully at the earliest opportunity. This approach doesn't have the same benefit of having a smaller income coming in for longer, but with the right planning it can work well.

The right option for you really depends on—you guessed it—*you*. The path you choose will dictate the approach you take around transitioning your investments from a growth to an income focus, the tax impact of restructuring your investments and what income you need to be drawing from your investments at any point in time.

No matter which path you choose, the impact of the choices you make at this stage of your journey will be significant and long lasting. Because you're working towards an end point where you may choose never to work (and earn) again, it's crucial you make the smartest moves at each point here.

I'll talk more about how you can tackle this, but given the importance of the decisions you'll be making here I strongly suggest seeking out some quality professional financial advice so you make the most out of what you have and end up in the strongest position possible.

Choose your wealth-building weapons

The key to making the best decisions for you on this journey is relatively simple, though not always easy. At any point in your journey, you need to understand the different pathways open to you.

There are seven options to grow your assets: you can save cash, buy shares, buy crypto, pay down debt, buy an investment property, buy your own home or contribute to your super. Figuring out your options isn't rocket science.

The tricky part is knowing which options to use when on your money journey. For most people, a combination of these wealth-building options will work best, and this combination will change as your money position evolves.

The best money and investing option for you has three main drivers: first, how much money it will make you; second, the risks involved in pursuing that course (how those risks can be managed and how you feel about the risk that's left over); and last but definitely not least, what the money move means for your ability to live the lifestyle you want.

How much money you'll make from an investment is important, but it's not the only important thing. If an investment will make you a heap of money but mean you're so stressed about the risk that you can't sleep at night, it's unlikely to be the best option for you. Similarly, a great investment that forces you to make drastic lifestyle sacrifices is unlikely to be the best investment for you.

To make the best choice for you, it's important you first understand the financial impact of the different potential pathways. What would it mean for your money trajectory if you save in cash vs buy shares vs buy property vs pursue any other course? Of course, the financial impact of the different options will differ.

Then you need to look at what's not in the numbers. Understand the risk you're facing, for example by committing to making a monthly mortgage repayment vs having a regular ETF investment plan in place that you can pause at any time. Or the risk of interest rates increasing on your investment properties vs the risk of locking money away in your super fund. Or the risk of not generating income from your crypto portfolio to target a higher return vs the consistency of an index fund investment.

Each of these risks will naturally feel a little different for you. Some will make you more comfortable than others. Some will make you feel so uncomfortable they just won't be right for you.

It's valuable to explore all options, even if you know that one or more won't be right for you. Exploring an option and then ruling it out gives you a different level of peace of mind compared with just thinking an option isn't right but not exploring it fully.

Fear > inaction > missed opportunities

It's natural to be fearful of things you don't understand, and fear is the single biggest roadblock to investing as much as you could or should. The fear of making a mistake that will cost you a bunch of money is very real. You want to invest but are unsure of certain elements and their impact. This uncertainty grows into concern, which then builds into fear, and before you know it you're paralysed.

Fear is natural and healthy—it will prevent you from doing something dumb that will cost you a bunch of money. But if you let it, fear can also stop you from playing a bigger game and getting bigger results. The safe option is the known option, the one that comes with the lowest level of risk. But it's also the option that will make you the least amount of money.

Saving money in a bank account feels amazing. You can see it building, you know the money is immediately accessible if you need it. You know it can't go backwards. But cash is also the lowest returning investment of all the asset-building options you can take. And it too is a risk, although most people don't recognise this.

I don't advocate being reckless towards risk, but there's a position somewhere between the two extremes that's right for you. Locating this position will help you build more investments sooner and make faster progress. Find it!

A word of advice here. Don't let the fact you don't fully understand investments and the risk that comes with them stop you from making a choice. Take the time to understand your different asset- and wealth-building options, their impact, their risks and the trade-offs so you can make the best choice for you — one you can be confident to act on. You want to make your choice from a position of confidence, not one of uncertainty or fear.

You can educate yourself in many ways, including by reading this book, doing online research and learning by doing. But if you're considering bigger moves that will have a significant impact on your financial situation into the future, one way to accelerate your education around risks and how to manage them is getting good professional help.

If you're early on your journey to replace your salary by investing, this can give you the support you need to make some solid decisions and set your direction for the years to come. If you're further along, advice can help you make sense of your options and get more out of what you have today. Once you choose the best path forward for you, you can be confident that you've made the very best choice and will be much more likely to follow through with full conviction to get the results you want.

How to crunch your numbers

A lot of magic comes from mapping out the financial pathway you're on. When you do this right, you establish a baseline for the outcomes you can expect moving forward.

If you keep doing exactly what you're doing today, you'll get a solid sense of how your money will grow and where you should be in a month, a year or 10 years. Importantly, you'll also be able to determine the financial impact of making any changes to your plan.

You can look at the impact if you were to increase your rate of savings or your regular investment plan, what it would look like if you were to purchase an investment property, how your existing investment property would grow and when your property equity will have increased to the point where you can purchase your next investment property.

When you're in the early stages of your journey to replace your salary, things will likely be fairly simple. You won't have a lot of investments, assets or debts that you need to factor in, so calculating out your trajectory should be relatively straightforward.

Your main focus at this point will probably be investing with shares, most likely through a micro-investing platform. In this case, all you really need is a compound interest calculator and maybe a spreadsheet. I suggest using the ASIC Moneysmart compound interest calculator, which is free and easy to use. If you want some tips on using this tool you can access a free video at pivotwealth.com.au/rsi/, where I talk through how best to use this calculator.

When planning your investments, start with what you think you can save and invest today. But I'd strongly recommend you at least look at the impact if you were to increase how much you're investing even slightly. You'll likely be surprised by the impact, and this might just give you the extra motivation you need to find a way to increase your savings rate.

Over time, as your situation evolves, mapping out your money will become more complex, particularly when you start including property, mortgages, superannuation and different strategies to help with your tax planning. Unfortunately this isn't something a simple compound interest calculator can deliver. It's also tricky to map out in a spreadsheet—on your own.

Financial planners use special software that factors in all the different tax rules and allows someone to focus on different elements of a money strategy and assess the impact of taking different pathways from where you are to where you want to be.

This software isn't yet publicly available, and even if it was, it probably wouldn't be the best idea to try to figure it all out on your own. As I've noted, the rules are complex, and the impact of big money choices over time is likely to be measured in the hundreds of thousands of dollars (or millions).

This means even if you were able to access the software you probably wouldn't be able to arrive at a point where you would be certain nothing had been missed and have total confidence to execute on bigger moves without having someone supporting you in this process.

As you start to make bigger moves on your money journey, you should look closely at getting quality financial advice to map out your best pathway forward. This will help you take a robust and comprehensive approach to understanding your options, and will deliver the confidence you need to go all-in on your chosen pathway forward.

THE WRAP

I've mentioned a couple of times that the stages to replacing your salary are simple, but putting them into practice isn't. The devil is in the detail here. To make the most out of what you have today and what you'll build into the future, to find the line of least resistance to replacing your salary by investing, you need to take a smart approach.

The opportunity here is huge.

When you get your game plan right, you'll create a clear pathway from where you are today to the ideal money results you want for the future, delivered in a timeframe you're happy with. This will deliver true financial confidence and peace of mind, and guarantee you avoid financial stress and worry.

Just as importantly, you'll be clear on the tactics needed for you to get the most out of the money you have today and avoid taking on the wrong risks while living the lifestyle you really want.

It's worth working for.

Your action plan

- Take the time to understand how your investment choices need to deliver good investment results *and* fit in with the lifestyle you want to live.

- Understand your wealth-building weapons and which ones are right for where you're at today on your journey to replace your salary by investing.

- Educate yourself or seek professional advice to overcome investing fear and build the confidence to take action.

- Map out your current financial 'baseline' and financial trajectory.

- Build on your baseline to assess the impact of different investments and saving and investing at different rates.

- Choose the investment approach that gives you the best balance between financial results, risk and lifestyle.

- Incorporate your tax planning *before* you invest.

- Take action!

CHAPTER 9

DIY, get help or procrastinate

It's easy to fall into the trap of thinking your goal is to make 'good' money choices. There's a heap of information (and noise) out there on what makes a good investment, how to make good property choices, how to choose a good super fund and how to be good at saving.

But unfortunately 'good' isn't *enough*.

The people I talk to about their money want it all. They want to be able to afford their dream home without a crippling mortgage. They want an epic lifestyle. They want investment income so they don't feel trapped in their job. And they want the ability to support the people and causes they care about.

These things don't come cheap. We're lucky to live in one of the most amazing countries in the world, but living well in Australia is expensive, which means if you want the freedom to live well, you need to have the money to back it up.

To get there, you need to make the 'best' choices for you. This is what will allow you to optimise your money and maximise every opportunity to get the most out of what you have now. If you're not a money expert already, though, you often don't know what you don't know.

Most people think that choosing good investments is *the* key to being successful with money. As I've noted, choosing good investments is important, but it's only one part of the picture.

True money success means:

- choosing good investments
- investing the right amount at the right time
- being smart with tax
- using the ideal amount of debt and leverage for you
- adopting the ideal property strategy
- setting good goals and targets
- managing your risk
- being smart with your debt
- using expert frameworks.

Money success has many layers. Sometimes your next steps are obvious, but there are always more to come, and if you aren't thinking three steps ahead you can sometimes make choices you'll later come to regret.

It is absolutely possible for anyone to learn enough about money to get some good results on their own. But it will take you hundreds of hours of research, and years of trial and error. You'll learn through costly mistakes and setbacks. If you're sufficiently dedicated and put in the work, you will eventually get there, but it will be slow going, because mistakes and missed opportunities will inevitably slow your progress.

Early momentum compounds into serious dollars

When it comes to money, as I've unpacked in previous chapters particularly around investing, your initial momentum is a big driver of the results you'll get over time.

Time and money are beautiful things — when they're on your side.

When you let time pass without taking action you lose an opportunity. We've all been there, kicking ourselves for not pulling the trigger on that share purchase, pushing to make a property purchase happen, or maybe even just being better with our budgeting and saving.

Looking back, it seems like such an obvious move, but we let life get in the way and pay the price. And the real cost of missed opportunity isn't just the amount of money we didn't make at the time we were thinking about taking action. The lost opportunity is that when we don't take action, we won't be quite as far along 12 months from today. But the *real* cost is the growth that extra money would compound to create for us years into the future.

For example, just $5000 invested using the long-term Australian share market return of 9.8 per cent would be worth $248 022 in 40 years' time. This means *every single year* you don't take action you're potentially costing yourself almost a quarter of a million dollars. When you add that opportunity cost over years into the future, the impact is huge.

It's common for people to decide to get on the front foot with their money. I hope reading this book has motivated you to act on this decision.

You're excited as you plan your next steps, and the momentum starts to build. You decide to set up some investments, but you're finding the options confusing, and you don't want to make a mistake, so you figure you need to do some more research before you get started. Then life gets in the way, you get distracted, more time passes and before you know it you're stalled again.

I see this a lot in the financial planning work we do at Pivot Wealth, where at the start of the year we always chat to a heap of people who are full of new year's resolution. They come to us determined to make this the year they finally take action.

But over the years I've noticed a trend. Some of these people lean in and get started, but a significant group become distracted and drift off track. We wind up having the same conversations with them next year (sometimes even multiple years). Eventually they get things sorted, but *every single person* regrets not getting started sooner.

DIY, get help, get good help or delay

At this point you only have four options when it comes to taking action with your money:

- You can do it yourself.
- You can get some help.
- You can get *good* help.
- You can procrastinate.

Do it yourself

If you're really interested in building your money and have time to do all the research yourself, taking this approach can lead to serious growth of your money muscle over the long term.

The downside is the time cost, and the fact you have to learn through trial and error, making mistakes that slow your progress. As mentioned above, the cost of slower progress over the next few years will compound to a loss of big bucks (at least into the hundreds of thousands of dollars), so tread carefully here.

You can get some help

Having someone in your corner can help you build confidence and take action with your money, saving you a heap of time and frustration in the process.

You can get *good* help

There's a difference between getting help and getting good help. Having someone to help with your money can really motivate you. But having someone give you truly good help with your money can deliver the best *results* given the position you're in today.

Of course I'm completely biased, because this is what we do through our financial planning work at Pivot Wealth. But I know that getting the best help behind you from step 1 will mean you get ahead faster by taking advantage of every opportunity to get more out of your money.

Keep in mind that the real measure of paying someone for help with your money is how much money they will make you. I unpack this in detail in this chapter, but if you're thinking about getting someone to help with your money, take the time to understand the financial upside they can deliver and consider this alongside the cost of their support. This will help you establish the real financial 'cost' of getting help, which is likely to be a net positive one.

You can procrastinate

Money is one of those things that is important but often not urgent. It's easy for it to be pushed onto the backburner, put off to a tomorrow that never seems to come around. The cost of going down this path is the opportunity cost of not taking the smartest actions now, which compounds every year—forever. I don't recommend you choose this option.

Where is the actual benefit in financial advice

There are three main areas where financial advice delivers value.

The first is *non-quantifiable benefits*: confidence, a feeling of financial wellbeing, saving you time, keeping you accountable and protecting you from risks that aren't always clear to you. Non-quantifiable benefits do have financial benefits attached to them, but they can be hard to pin down.

For example, say you've thought about investing but are nervous about making a bad investment and losing money. If you try to figure it all out on your own, you can spend a heap of time doing research before finding an investment and pulling the trigger to get started.

In this case, it probably would have taken you longer to get to the trigger point. You might then invest a smaller amount of the money you have available to 'test the waters' and get comfortable. And your regular investments moving forward might also be a little smaller as you build confidence in the pathway you've chosen.

If, instead, you found a really good financial adviser to guide you through the process of shaping your investment strategy and choosing your options, to educate you about the risks and how they can be managed, which account would be best based on your circumstances, and then help you to set up the accounts so they're ready to rock, you're in an altogether better position.

You're likely to have more confidence to invest more money initially, and you'll probably be more motivated to invest more moving forward. The result is you'll invest more money sooner, which through compounding will deliver a substantial upside to the investment results you get over time.

The real impact of the difference between the DIY option and having solid professional help is that you'll be investing more money overall and, importantly, more money sooner. And by now you know enough to know that this will result in more growth, which will compound every year for the rest of your life.

There's a clear benefit here, but it's hard to quantify in dollar terms.

In addition, you have benefits such as the peace of mind of knowing you're on track to replace your salary by investing on a timeline you're happy with, the confidence the risks that are really important to you are being managed, and a reduction in stress and frustration knowing you have someone to do the heavy lifting for you.

All these benefits are hard to attach a dollar value to, but for most people they offer a heap of value, benefits I feel are as valuable, or even more valuable, than the actual financial upside you'll receive from financial advice.

Nevertheless, I totally understand that when you're thinking about investing money in financial advice you want to understand the measurable return on your investment (ROI) you can expect for these fees.

When you get financial advice, there are two areas that will drive this ROI: the 'value of advice' and your 'advice upside'.

Value of advice

Value of advice is a term I use to capture all the immediate, quantifiable benefits you receive from financial advice. A list of these areas would include:

- tax savings from investment structuring or restructuring
- fee savings on financial products such as investment accounts, super funds and insurance premiums
- tax savings from super contributions
- investment growth from investing savings or using property equity to invest
- increasing your rate of savings
- tax savings on debt recycling strategies
- savings on interest costs from mortgages or personal debt
- financial uplift from employer share plan strategies.

Implementing these strategies and tactics will provide you with an immediate financial benefit, often one that continues to be received every single year into the future.

Typically, the benefits from this area will far outweigh the cost of financial advice in year 1 alone. The benefit for the years ahead goes straight to your bottom line as pure profit.

Advice upside

At Pivot, we're a bit anal about tracking client results. One way we do this is by projecting how our clients' financial position will progress over time based on what they're doing when they come to us compared with the financial trajectory they choose to follow after going through our planning process.

We call this *advice upside*. It is the benefit you will receive over time by following through on the strategies, investments and tactics in your financial plan. We've calculated that for our average client through 2021 the advice upside figure averaged $71 203 per annum.

Relating this back to the power of compounding, if you were to invest $71 203 into the share market today, assuming the average share market return of 9.8 per cent, this money would compound to be worth $1 330 879 in 30 years' time. This is the upside from *one year alone*.

And here's the thing: the average annual benefit is something you'll receive *every single year*.

Results are everything

An adviser who plays at the surface level can make you feel really good about your money but won't deliver results. When searching for an adviser, look for someone who starts with the end in mind, someone with a clear focus on the results you want, and who builds every part of the advice process to make these results happen.

Good advice shouldn't be a cost but a profit centre. Sure, you could use an average advice company that delivers average results and save a few bucks. A lot of people fall into this trap through their focus on the cost of advice alone.

Most of these people come to learn that they eventually have to unwind or reset their strategy, an exercise that often costs more than how much you spent on cheap advice. Then there's the opportunity cost of lost time you'll never get back.

It seems simple when you look at it, but in assessing the cost of any option you need to factor in the cost of advice *and* the money you'll make from taking that advice — the 'net cost'.

So long as the cost of the advice is lower than the net benefit you'll receive from the advice, you're ahead.

Types of financial advice

When seeking financial advice, it's essential you know what sort of advice you're looking for. If you don't, you won't get the right outcomes from the advice process. You may not solve the issues or get the results you want. You can also waste a bunch of time and become frustrated as you go through the process.

When you're clear on the sort of advice you want or need, you'll get a better outcome from your advice process, save time and frustration, and ultimately give yourself a much better chance of getting the financial results that are important to you.

Sometimes you might need advice in a specific area; other times you might be looking for general advice to get the most out of your situation. It's critical to understand the difference, and know what sort of advice you want or need *before* you start looking.

For example, imagine you have saved or inherited $50 000 and just want an adviser to help you build an investment strategy for this money and not look at the rest of your situation. This very specific need would result in specific advice, sometimes called *scaled advice*.

The alternative option is broader in scope. You might have $50k that you want to do something smart with, but you want to confirm what investment strategy is best and how it fits with your broader financial strategy. You also want to know how best to find your next $50k (and the one after that) to add to your investments, as well as any other things you can be doing to get more out of your money. This is called *comprehensive advice* or 'comprehensive planning'.

The distinction between them may sometimes seem small, but there is an enormous difference in the output. Understanding this difference is the first step to getting the outcomes you want from financial advice.

In the case of specific advice, your adviser is only helping you invest money. If you ask an adviser for this type of advice, they will let you know their advice is limited to how best to invest your money and isn't considering any other aspect of your financial situation.

What this means is your adviser isn't advising whether investing is the very best thing to be doing with your money. They aren't reviewing your plans to invest relative to your other goals and the lifestyle you want to live, and your adviser isn't exploring whether there are other opportunities to get more out of the financial position you're in today.

In the second instance, your adviser is helping with your investment plan as part of your overall financial and lifestyle strategy. Comprehensive advice means your adviser:

- is required to build up a full understanding of your overall financial situation
- will explore if investing is the very best thing to do with this money
- offers advice that is not limited to investing your money, but covers investing as part of your overall strategy and will help you understand the implications of your investment
- is obligated to raise any issues, risks, roadblocks or potential problems with your investment strategy with reference to your other targets or goals
- will discuss any opportunities or issues in other areas of your financial situation (outside of your investment strategy) and help you understand how you can take advantage of these opportunities.

Scaled advice will help you answer one specific question or address one particular issue. On the other hand, comprehensive advice will deliver an outcome that helps you:

- cut through information overload to set up a clear strategy
- find the ideal balance between getting ahead with money and living the lifestyle you want

- build confidence to overcome your fear of making a mistake and taking action, because you know absolutely everything has been considered
- optimise your tax strategy to increase your after-tax investment return
- map out an achievable pathway to replace your salary by investing in a timeframe you're happy with
- choose the best investments to grow your wealth
- set up a banking structure to make it easier for you to save more money
- protect your key risks and downsides.

Specific advice has its place. It's best when you're 100 per cent sure a particular strategy is the very best thing for you to be doing and you just need help in executing it. But in my experience, it can be hard to be 100 per cent confident a specific approach is going to be the absolute best thing for you *without* being a personal finance expert yourself.

The outcome of comprehensive advice should be to help you set up a clear, easy-to-follow plan from where you are today to the money and lifestyle outcomes you want. Comprehensive advice will be more detailed, need more inputs, take a little longer to put together and cost more, but it will go further in helping you to actually achieve your money goals.

Comprehensive advice is more suitable for those still building their money knowledge who don't yet know all the possibilities for getting more out of their money and who are still building a pathway to their goal. If this sounds like you, it's important you take the time to explore your options and decide which specific path is the right one for you. This will give you the confidence to take action and clarity on the direction you're taking, which in turn will mean you're more likely to stick with your strategy because you know it's the very best one for you.

In my view, your overall plan should drive the specific strategies you follow and investments you make, not the other way around. As we discussed in the previous chapter, making 'good' choices in isolation can lead to suboptimal outcomes.

Make sure you get clear on the type of advice you want before you start the process. This will drive the sort of advice you seek and will help you ask the right questions to get the right results.

Which financial adviser will make you the most money

The way I see it, the job of a financial adviser is to help people cut through the noise.

The weird thing is that, with over 16 000 financial advisers in Australia, all doing things a bit differently, figuring out who will be the right people to help you can in itself feel overwhelming. Here I'll unpack the key things you need to understand before choosing the best adviser for you.

These are the top three questions you should be asking your potential adviser:

- What is your experience in helping people in a similar financial position to me?'
- What are the sorts of financial results I can expect from your advice?
- How do you charge, and do you receive any conflicted payments or kick-backs that could influence the advice you might give me?

You need an expert on your particular problems

Question 1 will help give you confidence that this adviser is an expert on the challenges you're facing and the opportunities available to you.

This element is crucial, because whether you fully recognise or understand the problems, challenges and opportunities you're facing, they will be significant. And solving them *is* valuable.

When you find an adviser with deep experience working with other people in a similar position to you, they will have expert knowledge on your problems. They'll be familiar with the mistakes people in similar situations have made so can help you avoid them.

They'll also know about the hidden opportunities that can help you get ahead faster and be able to share the hacks and tactics that will increase your chances of getting the results you want in the shortest time possible.

Plans are your pathway to results

Question 2 is designed to show you how 'results focused' your adviser is. It's common for advisers to get super-excited about building your financial plan, but what's sometimes lost is the fact that your plan is only one way to get you the outcomes you want—extra dollars in your savings account, growth in your investments and wealth, or progress buying your dream home and clearing your mortgage.

While it's impossible to know specifically what financial results you'll get from putting a good financial plan into place before you actually put it together, a good adviser should be able to show you how they measure the true impact of their advice through things like your value of advice and advice upside, as already outlined. This will give you some insight into what the upside is likely to look like for you.

Fees are important, but not just because of the cost

Question 3 will confirm two things: whether they're going to charge enough to actually deliver the results you want; and whether there are any conflicts of interest that have the potential to influence your advice.

There's no one right way here, but it's important you understand the different ways advisers can charge and their potential impact. At Pivot we believe a 'fee for service' model is the most transparent way to charge, meaning we're paid a fixed dollar fee for the services we offer.

We don't get paid according to whether you buy shares or property, crank your super or choose just to save money in a bank account. We take this approach to give our clients confidence that we're motivated only by making sure they're stoked with the plan we help them create, so they choose to keep working with us for a long time, and tell all their mates.

With a fee for service model, the fees will be higher than another company that's paid kickbacks from other products, services or related businesses. But with other models you often end up paying more—it's just that the fees are hidden. This will often cost you more in the long run.

You should want to pay a lot for your advice

I talk to more people than I'd like to who have paid for financial advice but haven't received the results they were looking for. Most of the time, when we talk it through it becomes clear they weren't paying enough to get the outcome they wanted.

The simple reality is, if your adviser says they're going to deliver you the world and do it on the cheap, they either aren't going to deliver, or they're going to have to lose money to deliver. Neither option is sustainable.

When you choose a premium advice option, you'll have a solution where your adviser is charging enough to put in the time and work needed to deliver on their service promises.

Cheap financial advice will typically cost you much more than the price you actually pay. This cost comes from not getting the results you wanted, not investing as much as you could or should have sooner, and not having the level of support needed to drive your ideal results.

Ten questions you should ask your potential adviser

I have introduced you to the top three questions you should ask any prospective adviser and why they're important. Following is a longer list of key questions you can use when screening an adviser. Their answers should give you a good sense of the adviser and advice business you're considering partnering with.

1. What is your experience working with people like me?
2. What sort of results should I expect from your advice and where will I see the value?
3. How do you charge and are you paid in any other ways — that is, through product or referral fees, or payments from related businesses or businesses you have commercial relationships with?
4. How much of your help involves me making decisions vs you telling me what will be best?
5. How do you balance lifestyle and financial goals in your planning and advice?
6. Where does education fit into your advice process?
7. What do you do in the initial planning stages to ensure my plan translates into results?
8. What do you do through your ongoing service to ensure I'm getting the results I've planned for?
9. How do you choose the products you recommend for your clients?
10. How will you track my progress through the plan we create?

The adviser's responses should give you some good insights into how aligned their approach is with what you're looking for and the confidence to move forward.

How to choose an adviser

Understanding the issues covered in this chapter will help you screen advisers and make the right choice for you. Here I'll put this together to help you build a shortlist of advisers to screen.

A good place to start your research is talking to people in your network about any good experiences they've had with financial advisers. When doing this, you should put more weight on the responses of people who are in a similar position to yourself.

For example, if you're chatting with colleagues at the office who are at a similar stage in their career and life (and have a similar income) to you, their suggestions will carry more weight than those of a mate or family member who you know is at a very different stage in their financial life.

Other financial professionals you're already working with, such as accountants, mortgage brokers and property people, can be a useful resource here, though it's important to keep in mind the sort of advice and service you're receiving from them.

You can also do some research online through Google and social media. Rather than searching for 'financial advice Sydney' or 'best financial advisers', though, I suggest looking for answers and content on the specific problems you're trying to solve.

For example, if you're just getting started with your money you might search around 'how to get started investing' or 'how ETFs work'. If you're looking more strategically at your tax, you might look at 'how to save tax when investing' or 'how to reduce my tax bill'.

Taking this approach to your search will likely lead you to experts in the specific problems or opportunities you seek advice on.

Following the steps I've outlined, you should be able to create a shortlist of advisers who might be able to help you and then screen them to find the best one to deliver the results you want.

Even if you think you're not ready for advice, I recommend taking the time to do some research and have some conversations with potential advisers. This way you'll be able to ask advisers directly how they think they'll be able to help you, and when they think you should get started with financial advice.

Most good advice businesses are happy to spend some time chatting to people they think might benefit from their help in the future, even if the time isn't right now. We do this out of goodwill and relationship building, and we know that someone today might just need a couple of tips and things to focus on to accelerate their progress to a point where they're likely to need more significant help.

Any time you invest here will be well spent, even if you don't take up formal financial advice immediately.

Screen 1: Content and philosophies

There are a few things to look for at this stage. First, you should look for content the adviser has put out so you can get a sense of their advice philosophies and approach. As I've reiterated a few times in this book, there are a lot of different ways to be right when it comes to money.

When seeking out your adviser, make sure the things they think are important are aligned with the things you think are important, and that the way they explain money concepts makes sense to you.

When checking out their content—written, video, audio or any combination—look for transparency in their views and make sure they align with yours.

Screen 2: Size and support

Financial plans are nothing more than a tool to help you achieve financial results. It sounds a little counterintuitive, but when you seek out advice your plan is important but it's not really the most important thing.

When looking at a potential adviser, you want to make sure they have the support and systems in place to turn your awesome financial plan into great financial outcomes. There's only so much one person can do alone, so your adviser will need good support around them—specifically their team, tech and business resources.

To ensure you'll be well supported, look for advice businesses that have a solid team around them and the right tech to support you.

Look for a team around your adviser who will be tasked with getting you the outcomes you want from your process. I know there are a lot of great micro-advice businesses out there, but typically, as these businesses grow and mature, something has to give. You don't want to be on the wrong side of this equation.

You should also ask your adviser how many clients they personally look after, and whether there is a cap on the number of clients they plan to take on. Again, one person can only do so much.

Screen 3: Track record

Look for an advice business that has runs on the board. Check customer reviews and testimonials to get a feel for what other people are saying. While most reviewers won't be disclosing the granular detail of what's going on with their money, you should get a sense of the position they're in and what help they received to ensure it aligns with what you're looking for.

You can also look for external validation of the model through awards and external recognition. Awards and external recognition aren't everything. I fully appreciate there are a number of great businesses that go unrecognised, so it's not to say that a business that hasn't won a heap of awards can't be great. But such recognition does say something about the adviser or business you're assessing.

For myself, I make sure that each year Pivot Wealth participates in a number of awards programs, because it forces us to think more deeply about our advice model. It leads us to focus on the elements of what we do that deliver the most value for our customers. It highlights any gaps or issues that need to be addressed and helps us to get clear on the things we're doing to continuously improve.

It's easy to put great marketing spin on something that's not so great. But it's another thing to have a panel of experts scrutinise your approach by shining a light on the seen and unseen areas of a business.

When screening your potential adviser, look at what types of external validation they have of their model and think about what this means for you.

Screen 4: Relationships and products

When your adviser has a relationship with another company that provides products or services, particularly where taking up those products or services creates a financial benefit for your adviser, a conflict is created.

The two most common examples are where your adviser or advice company is owned by or linked to a financial product provider such as a super fund or investment manager, or where they have a relationship with other businesses in or around the property space.

This kind of arrangement used to be much more common when the banks were heavily involved in the financial advice space, where they employed armies of financial advisers to sell their products. As the saying goes, 'when your only tool is a hammer everything looks like a nail', and there's no doubt large numbers of people were sold products that in hindsight weren't the best option for them.

When your advice company has an interest in your adopting a particular solution, whether it's a super fund, investment account or property, and they're paid accordingly, it can lead them to make the solution fit when it's not necessarily the best thing for you. Even when it is, if your adviser is conflicted you're likely to lack confidence in their advice.

One of the biggest benefits of taking up good-quality financial advice is that you build total confidence in the pathway you're following with your money. I don't believe this can be achieved where a significant conflict exists.

It's common for people seeking advice not to realise that a conflict exists until they are a long way in. I see this happen more commonly than I'd like. People chat with an adviser and feel like everything is going well, only to realise when they actually receive their financial advice that there's a big conflict of interest.

When this happens, you have two choices: either you push on with the advice and hope for the best, despite your concerns, doubt and stress; or you seek out alternative advice, meaning the time and money spent on going through the first process was likely wasted.

Ask the questions about how your adviser is paid and how they charge at the front end to avoid nasty surprises later on.

Screen 5: Money vs lifestyle focus

I've saved the best for last. The *real* reason people go down the path of seeking advice is to help them live their ideal lifestyle and set up the future they want. If you have an adviser who focuses only on the dollars and not on the life you want to live around your money, you can run into problems.

If you're looking for a money plan that will work for you in the long term, you'll need one that helps you get ahead financially at the rate you want while at the same time you live the lifestyle you want. Ask your adviser how they'll help you find that balance.

THE WRAP

Financial advice can help you achieve your goals faster. But this only works if the advice you get is the right advice for you, where you're at today and what you're looking to do with your money.

You will more than likely seek advice at some point, and if you're committed to getting the most out of your money you'll probably do it sooner rather than later. Even if you're not in the market for financial advice today, you should understand how it works and what you should look out for.

This way you'll understand what, when and how advice can help you at different stages on your journey to replace your salary by investing, and how to choose the best adviser to get you the results you want from your money.

Your action plan

☐ Focus on the power and impact of early investing momentum, and how much money this can make you over time.

☐ Understand the four options for taking action with your money covered in this chapter—DIY, get help, get good help or procrastinate.

☐ Get clear on the benefits, quantifiable and non-quantifiable, of financial advice.

☐ Understand the different types of financial advice you can access and when each might be right for you.

☐ Take the time to think through what sort of adviser will best deliver the optimal financial results.

☐ Understand financial advice fees, how advisers charge, and what sort of charging model makes the most sense for you.

☐ Build your adviser screening questions.

☐ Create a shortlist of advisers or advice businesses you think might be able to help you, either now or in the future.

☐ Start a conversation with one or more advisers, even if you're not yet ready to sign up.

Your next steps

That's a wrap! In this book I've covered the building blocks of your money success, and how to put them together in a way that will help you replace your salary by investing while you live a lifestyle you love.

It might all seem almost too simple, but that doesn't mean it's easy. If you want to achieve true money success, you have to put in the work to get there.

While there's no one path to money success that will work for everyone, there's one approach *you* can take to find the perfect money pathway for you.

You have to build good habits

Choosing good investments is just one important factor that drives how quickly you get ahead with your money. Others are being smart with tax, making good money choices and managing your risk — and the list goes on.

Ultimately, though, the money habits and behaviours you build will have the greatest impact on your rate of financial progress. Building good habits and behaviours around saving and investing, reviewing your progress, setting goals and thinking about your money management are all crucial to achieving your financial potential.

It's terrific to have great ideas and great plans for your money. But ideas won't make you rich, and plans without action are worthless. Action drives results, so you have to make it happen. But taking action is scary when you're facing a lot of unknowns, which means you need to educate yourself before you can take *confident* action.

Reading this book is a great start. I hope it has given you the confidence to make your next move. If not, take the time to understand what you need to do to get there — *then* make it happen.

Remember, you don't need to be an expert today, because you'll build your money skills and knowledge over time. You just need to know enough to take the next step. Learn from what you're doing now so you can take another step to building your money momentum. Before you know it, your momentum will be doing the heavy lifting for you, making it easier to get better results in less time.

Saving and spending is your foundation

Budgeting and banking are the least sexy part of your money strategy, but they are the foundation on which *everything* else is built. If you don't get these right, you'll always be fighting an uphill battle.

Worst case, you'll be forced to sell investments at the wrong time and suffer financial setbacks. Perhaps even worse, if you aren't nailing it with your spending and saving, you'll constantly fall short of your financial potential and end up trapped in money mediocrity.

The best saving and spending strategy is the one that delivers you the perfect balance between your priorities of living the life you want today *and* saving at the rate you want for the future.

Everyone's priorities are different, so there is no 'perfect' amount to save or spend — there's only the approach that's perfect for you. What's important is that you're making your saving and spending choices with your eyes open.

Once you have a saving and spending plan you're happy with, you need a system to back it up. This will help you save more easily and automate your day-to-day money management, saving you a heap of time and improving the quality of your results.

Being on top of your money will go a long way to delivering peace of mind, eliminating financial stress and improving your financial wellbeing. Perhaps most important, being solid with your saving will give you confidence when investing. Knowing you have a savings system that's working well, you'll be able to invest aggressively and with total confidence.

Investing is your fuel on the journey

You'll never replace your salary by investing if you only save money in cash — you *have* to invest, and the sooner you get started, the better your results will be. Most people know they need to invest. But there's a difference between knowing something and acting on it, and the fear of making mistakes can be paralysing.

This fear comes from the unknown, but fear can be overcome by knowledge — understanding investments and investment risk and how it can be managed. Once you know your investing unknowns and have your risk managed, you're ready to rock.

When you invest, getting crystal clear on the investment trajectory you're on will give you confidence and motivation. A compound interest calculator is your friend here.

Always take the time to map out how your investments are likely to grow over time based on how much you're investing today. This will help you understand the results you should expect over time and give you the motivation to keep moving forward. You'll also understand the impact of investing more or less, allowing you to adjust and refine your strategy over time.

Remember, the best time to get started investing was 10 years ago, the second-best time is today.

Property is a winning strategy

When it comes to growing your investments and building your wealth, the only thing better than investing your money is investing with leverage. When you choose sound investments, using good, tax-effective debt to invest more sooner will ensure your investments grow faster.

It's simple maths, and the money is yours for the taking. But borrowing to invest significantly increases your risk levels, so it's crucial you manage your risk well to avoid trouble.

There are many myths out there around property, and much of the common 'wisdom' can send you down the wrong property path. Stick to the basics and you'll go a long way to ensuring your success.

Your decision around buying your own home is one that will have a significant and long-lasting impact on your rate of progress in getting ahead with your money. The right move at the wrong time is the wrong move, so tread carefully here.

Buying your dream home is an important part of true money success, and I know with certainty that it's achievable for you. But be sure to buy the *right* dream home at the *right* time.

Crypto can make you money, but you don't need it

With the meteoric rise of cryptocurrency, many people are asking themselves if they should be investing in crypto and digital assets. But the herd mentality can often push you towards making choices that are inconsistent with your other priorities.

There's no doubt in my mind that crypto has a future, but when that comes together and what it will look like is unclear at best. Stepping too far into the digital asset space before you get your foundational investment strategy on track would be a mistake that could be costly, both in terms of direct financial loss and the cost of compromising your other goals.

That said, digital assets can make sense as one element of a smart and considered investment strategy, and may potentially lead to some significant upside.

Whether or not you choose to invest in cryptocurrency and digital assets, you should seek to understand this space so you can make a considered choice. This way you'll be more confident in the path you've chosen, avoid second-guessing yourself and ultimately get the results you want without that niggling thought at the back of your mind that there's something you're missing that could cause you trouble down the track.

Super is your friend (but not your only friend)

There are a lot of myths surrounding super. Because the government has a tendency to tinker with the super rules, there's also a lot of distrust. And the fact that you can't touch your super for decades into the future leads many people to largely ignore it.

Superannuation is *your* money, and while your super fund might be managing it for you, I guarantee it isn't as important to them as it should be to you. This means *you* are the person who needs to be responsible for getting the most out of this money.

Superannuation is nothing more than an investment account with concessional tax treatment and some special rules. The tax rules are seriously tipped in your favour, with the tax on investment earnings and growth inside super being lower than on any other investment account. Tax deductions are available for making additional investments in your super. These factors increase the appeal of investing through super. It certainly shouldn't be ignored when you want to replace your salary by investing.

Super won't be your first go-to for investing, but it shouldn't be your last, and making small extra contributions over time will make a big difference to your future wealth.

By now you should understand that you can access any investment you'd want to buy outside of super inside the super environment, and that super isn't a special type of investment in and of itself.

Your investment strategy, preferences and philosophy should dictate which super fund you use, not the other way around. Set your investment strategy first, including your overall investment approach, which you can then apply to all your different investment accounts, super and non-super. Let the type of investments you want to hold dictate what super funds might be best for you to use to grow your superannuation investments.

Then give your super a little attention over time, checking in to make sure your money is doing what it should be doing and there isn't a better option out there for you.

Your after-tax investment return is all that matters

Tax is the silent killer, and because the rules are complicated and confusing it's easy for tax to hide underneath the surface. But every dollar of tax you save is an extra dollar you can use to replace your salary by investing faster.

When your investments are structured more tax effectively, you're able to generate a higher after-tax income from the same amount of wealth, so no matter where you want to end up you can get there faster.

There are many different strategies you can use to save tax, and you should have at least a basic understanding of each of them so you know when they can help you. But by far the biggest area for tax savings is around where you own your investments — whether that's in your name, your partner's name, joint names, or through superannuation or other tax entities.

It's expensive and time consuming to restructure your investments *after* you've put in the hard work and time to building them up, so understand the rules and how to use them to your advantage *before* you get started.

You need a game plan

The ideal money choices, investments and strategies for you depend on where you're at today, where you want to end up, what's likely to change over time and what's really important to you. There's no one set of steps to money success or replacing your salary by investing that will work for every single person, because the right moves for you depend on you.

But there is one approach to replacing your salary by investing and to your money decision making that *will* work for everyone. You need to understand where you're at now, what your options are, the impact of each of those options and how they fit in with the lifestyle you want to live.

By taking this approach, you can assess the financial upside or impact of different investments and how they fit with your personal goals and lifestyle. You can look at the impact of making changes to what you're doing today or what you're thinking about doing tomorrow, then make an informed choice about what will work best for you.

Most importantly, when you adopt this approach you have total confidence in the decisions you make, following them up with the action needed to get the results you want. And you have clarity on your financial trajectory, so you never have to worry about whether what you're doing will get you to where you want to be.

Financial advice will help you get there faster

As a financial adviser I'm clearly biased here, but I can say from my personal experience that getting good financial advice is a game changer that will accelerate how quickly you get ahead, the degree of confidence you have around your money plans, and your levels of financial and non-financial wellbeing.

I hope by now you have a much better understanding of your money and investment options. We've covered a lot of ground in this book, but in reality we've only really scratched the surface.

It's challenging to unpack two decades of investing experience, over a decade of formal study, and another decade plus of hands-on experience helping thousands of people with their financial advice and planning in a simple form that's easy to understand and to implement.

A good financial adviser can put their knowledge and experience to work for you, helping you understand your options and which are most relevant for you today. They can help you avoid the noise and distractions that don't move you forward. They can help you build better habits and avoid some of the money psychology traps that will hold you back. Importantly, they can also help you learn from the mistakes others have made so you can avoid making them yourself.

There is a cost attached to financial advice, but when you factor in the extra money you'll make, good financial advice will definitely give you a net benefit.

There are many different types of advice out there, so knowing which might be most helpful for you at which stage of your journey to replace your salary by investing is of great value to you.

Take the time to understand the fundamentals of financial advice and how and when it can benefit you, so you can take best advantage of it to fast-track your success. Your future self will thank you for it.

The wrap of wraps

Decision making around money can be hard, frustrating, even overwhelming. Getting it right takes lots of research, self-education and work, but the results are worth it. Money doesn't necessarily solve problems, but it does give you options — and without options you're trapped, no longer master of your own destiny.

I hope you've enjoyed reading this book as much as I enjoyed writing it. And I sincerely hope it has helped you understand more about the smart things you can do to navigate your money journey to true financial security and lifestyle freedom.

If you want to learn more about how you can implement the ideas in this book faster and easier, check out the tools and resources on our website: pivotwealth.com.au/rsi/, where you'll also find links to our podcast, live and online events, and social channels with a heap of other money tips, hacks and strategies to help you level up your money.

Remember, ideas without action are meaningless. So it's over to you to move things forward from here.

Ben

Index

Printed and bound by CPI Group (UK) Ltd, Croydon, CR0 4YY

20/03/2023

03203369-0001